Warming Up
to
Living Foods

Elysa Markowitz

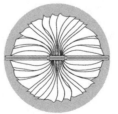

Book Publishing Company

Summertown, Tennessee

Distributed By:
Nature's First Law
POB 900202, SD, CA 92190
www.rawfood.com

Cover Photo: Dave Hawkins
Cover Design: Jeff Clark and Warren C. Jefferson
Interior Design: Warren C. Jefferson
Food Artist: Elysa Markowitz

Published in the United States by
Book Publishing Company
P.O. Box 99
Summertown, TN 38483
888-260-8458

10 09 08 07 06 05 04 03 02 01   2 3 4 5 6 7 8 9

ISBN 1-57067-065-X

Markowitz, Elysa
        Warming up to living foods / Elysa Markowitz
                p.   cm.
        Includes bibliographical references and index.
        ISBN 1-57067-065-X (alk. paper)
    1. Raw foods. 2. Cookery (Sprouts) 3. Cookery (Cold dishes)
4. Cookery, International. I. Title.
TX392.N26   1998
641.5'63--dc21   98-37160
                                                  CIP

The author is not responsible for any adverse effects or consequences resulting from the use of any of the preparations in this book. Please do not use the book if you are unwilling to assume the risk. Feel free to consult a physician or other qualified health professional. It is a sign of wisdom, not cowardice, to seek other opinions.

Not all of the flowers pictured in this book are edible. Please use them as a guide for adding a decorative touch to your meals, and consult a knowledgeable authority before eating any type of flower.

Table of Contents

Acknowledgements

In the process of writing this book there are several people who stand out as contributing to its inception, research, and writing. Initially I encountered the notion of warming up living foods from Deborah and Anthony Boyer who showed me how to use a dehydrator. Kim Sproul and Jamey Dina then sold me my first dehydrator and my Excalibur, which has been with me ever since. Johnny Lynch showed me how to use spices to warm up the food. And Ed Douglas certainly opened other doors to share additional concepts of using an electric skillet, and even the oven, on very low temperatures.

Preparing these dishes for workshops and dinners gave me feedback from many lovely folks. I thank them all for supporting me to experiment and do my research at Tree of Life Rejuvenation Center, where I prepared many warmed dishes throughout the winter months and got rave reviews from the folks there as well. I thank them for their appetites and kind words.

Darrell Price helped me prepare many of these meals and has enjoyed many of my food dishes. Thanks for all the help he provided over the last four years, lifting my stuff and moving the boxes of food and other supplies associated with my TV shows that shared with others how to warm up living foods.

Peter Stander provided me with a place to write the first draft of this book. Our exchange was rather unusual for him, but not so for me. I prepared him food and he gave me a quiet place to write in Silver City, New Mexico. A win-win situation for sure.

My printer, Ingram, at Superfast in Santa Monica, California, gave me an opportunity to share this book in its first stages with others by making it affordable and in form—not as lovely as this version, but I do think it helped many folks enjoy the concept of warming up a living food.

And I thank the folks who supported me in the workshops of the summer of 1997. Gloria and Paul Drnjezic of Bremerton, Washington, and Robin Sharan of the Annapurna Inn in Port Townsend, Washington, specifically. Their generous offer of home and hearth made it a joy and a pleasure to continue my raw food research.

Finally, when I went to create the photographs in Tennessee, I met Barbara Bloomfield and stayed at her bed and breakfast home. We played with how to lay out the food shots and created the gorgeous photographs that are in this book. Thank you again, Barbara, for your playful spirit, your ability to work with me, and the kindness you showed me during a time of stress.

And to Sharon Lockett for her editorial skills in reading this manuscript when I no longer could. She gave me constructive feedback as to how it could be a better book and held my hand through the final days of the completion of this process. The birth of a new book is completed.

And for it all, I thank Mother-Father God for the life I have and breathe and for the skills to continue to create and explore how to eat God's perfect foods. God bless you all.

Elysa Markowitz

Foreword

The title of this book, *Warming Up to Living Foods*, tells the whole story of the book and the significant contribution to the live food movement that Elysa Markowitz is making. This book shows how to make a creative and joyful transition to a live food cuisine.

Elysa's ability to artfully and tastefully combine tastes and texture with a multiplicity of interesting ingredients and international recipes takes her work to an exciting level of culinary joy. Her recipes are a sensual experience. In the time Elysa spent at the Tree of Life Rejuvenation Center in Patagonia, Arizona, I and my staff had a wonderful time enjoying the wide variety of tasty food that she prepared. Elysa's artful play of taste and textures is one of the key interesting elements of her food preparation cuisine. She does a nice job of communicating how to create the balance of live food taste and textures. It keeps the food interesting, attractive, and sensual in a way that makes it fun to eat. One can never say live foods are bland or boring after using these tastefully mouth-watering recipes.

One of the most important innovations in this book is Elysa's warm live foods recipes. The recipes in this book destroy the myth that live foods means cold foods. Live food enzymes and heat sensitive micro-nutrients do not begin to be destroyed until the temperature rises above 118°F. At 118°F, the solid or liquid is warm to the touch and brings heat into the body. Most foods are served too hot and we have to wait until they cool down to 118°F before we can eat them anyway. There are a variety of ways to warm foods besides warming them in a temperature-controlled crock pot. These include serving the food on a warm plate or pouring a hot sauce over a salad or other live food preparation.

One of the other important pieces of this book is Elysa's attention to the specific uses of different food preparation equipment. The way she describes how to use the different types of kitchen equipment makes working with live foods a lot easier for the person just entering into the live food cuisine experience. In fact, this book is extremely easy to use for the beginning live food preparer, as well as the experienced live food person. The design and layout of the recipes and explanations are well presented in a practical manner.

The most important reason to me for recommending this excellent and creative recipe book is that it tastefully and pragmatically shows how live foods can be prepared in ways that are appropriate for all seasons of the year and for a variety of different tastes and constitutions. The point I make in *Conscious Eating, Spiritual*

Nutrition, and *The Rainbow Diet* is that a live food cuisine is not just a cold salad, avocado, and sunflower seeds, but can be heating or cooling, building or detoxing, acidifying or alkalinizing, and adjusted to the season and one's psycho-physiological constitution. The live food diet as expressed in *Warming Up to Living Foods* is an expansion into health, well-being, and, as Elysa has so wonderfully shown, a new level of joyful and tasty eating.

We will be carrying this book at the Tree of Life Rejuvenation Center because we feel it will be a special help for those just starting on a live food lifestyle. It is well worth getting for everyone.

Blessings to your health,

Gabriel Cousens, M.D.
author of *Conscious Eating, Spiritual Nutrition*, and *The Rainbow Diet*
Director of The Tree of Life Rejuvenation Center, Patagonia, Arizona

Introduction

Warming Up To Living Foods is a unique approach to eating—a new paradigm in the way one could think of preparing food. Most raw foods books embrace a cold approach to eating living foods. This book is different. Now there is a choice to eat warm as well as frozen or cool. In fact, this approach is designed to encourage you to eat a warmed food every day, perhaps every meal.

This program will give you a choice; on the days you don't want to cook, you don't have to. No more greasy pots and pans to clean up afterwards.

Please don't assume that these foods are all cold or bland—oh, no. There are marinara sauces, spicy pâtés, warmed mousse, and piping warmed soups, as well as frozen desserts and other delights, cookies, and other foods you wished had more nutritious ingredients—now they do.

Warming Up To Living Foods is a blend of warmed, spiced, and texturized foods to impress you and your friends. Make a dish for them—don't tell them it's raw, just a new recipe. Here, taste this . . .

Warming Up To Living Foods contains seven days' worth of recipes: breakfast, lunch, dinner, desserts, snacks, and drinks. I would like to make one point very clear. I doubt that you could eat all these foods in one week; in fact, please don't try. I wouldn't. For example, all the food suggested for Day One does not have to be eaten on Day One. What you might do is make one meal, then prepare variations of that meal—so you don't have to go and buy a lot of different foods. Before you make the meals for the next day, check to see if anything needs soaking. Or would you rather do a day out of sequence? The order of the recipes is somewhat arbitrary; make them in any order you desire. Lunch could become dinner or the other way around. You could make a fruit meal for lunch or dinner or have vegetables for breakfast.

So just what is this cuisine—living foods? In this book, a living food is defined as a food that hasn't been heated over 105°F and has most, if not all, of its enzymes, vital substances for maintaining health and other life functions. Enzymes are essential for our health; virtually every important chemical reaction in our body is mediated by these special molecules. Digestion and assimilation are made possible by enzymes. If you want to know more about this fascinating topic, please read some of the references from the bibliography on page 137.

A living food is one that has been germinated or sprouted, is alive, like a grain or a nut or seed that has been soaked. A raw food is one that hasn't been sprouted, but has not been cooked either, such as any raw fruit or vegetable. It might be dehydrated, frozen, or prepared in such a way that most, if not all, of the enzymes are intact. In practical terms, it means that the food you eat will give you what you need to build health, not take it away.

Warming Up To Living Foods is about choices: a plethora of mouth-watering choices of what to do with grains, nuts, seeds, fruits, and vegetables—some you know and perhaps some will be new to you. There are concepts in this book that will show you the value of soaking or sprouting a food and how to marinate or ferment foods, and teach you other valuable skills to allow you to understand how to create even more recipes on your own. This book is intended to stretch your food imagination. You will learn how to create textures and tastes from familiar foods. You may never have made food in quite this way before. Let this seven days' worth of recipes grow into several years' worth of food preparation exploration. If I had been given this array of food choices when I first started eating living foods, I would have been a much happier camper.

My story started out on a very different path. I had watched my mother die of cancer, eaten my way from a size 8 to 16, and my health took a turn for the worse. I had to make a decision. I was experiencing arthritic symptoms—my neck, hip, and hands ached every day. I felt hypoglycemic—I would get very spaced-out if I ate too much fruit or if I went too long without eating. My cholesterol was over 245. I needed to stop what I was doing and re-evaluate my eating habits.

I was fortunate that I had several friends who helped me understand how to eat "raw" foods. In July of 1991, I started producing a public access television series and created raw and living food dishes. The first year I called the show *Meals in Minutes*; it then became *Live Food for Live People*, and is currently called *Elysa's Raw & Wild Food Show*. Occasionally I invite guests who share their information, recipes, and skills. Other shows highlight services or products that enhance or help create a healthier us, a healthier planet.

This book is the culmination of eight years of searching, researching, experimenting, and creating a new way to eat—a living foods approach.

Feel free to add spices, flavors, or foods you like. These recipes are intended to inspire, not imprison, you. I am the type of chef who loves to create new dishes and am not always concerned with the exact amounts of ingredients. I have tried my best to give you guidelines. But they are just that—guidelines—not the gospel.

Consider this approach for using this book. First, decide which menu or meal appeals to you. After you have eaten it, notice how you feel. One good sign that a food is agreeing with you is that you do *not* feel tired. Make variations on that meal using different ingredients or spicing it to your taste. After a while, choose another meal. Some of the ingredients may not be in season. Use those that are—for freshness and for maximum nutrients. For some people, oats are better for breakfast than fruit. For others, vegetables might fit the bill. Each person is special and unique. Listen to your body. If the nut dishes are too rich for you, stick with the vegetable entrees. I recommend that you eat your desserts separately, not after your meal. I have found that eating desserts after a meal often creates indigestion. Try eating your dessert on its own, an hour or more before a meal or several hours after a meal, not with it. Snacks might be an appetizer for a meal or an alternative to salad. Juice is a wonderful "cocktail" before any meal. Please don't drink it with your meal, as this tends to dilute your digestive juices and makes a soup out of any meal.

If you enjoy more of a particular spice, use it. If you don't like a particular spice, don't use it. Substitute one you do like. A word of caution—spice frugally at first, then add more. Adding is always easier than taking it out—once a flavor is there, it's there to stay.

For all the reasons you might have for eating, give these recipes a taste. Whether it is to lose weight, feel more energy, improve your health, or just to taste something different—start. Eat this style for a week, and see how you feel. Your bowels might move more. You might even feel lighter. Decide how you want to start, and bon appetite.

Getting Started

Simply put, you'll enjoy having five machines in your living foods kitchen:

- a juicer,
- a blender,
- a dehydrator,
- an electric skillet,
- and a food processor.

Here is some information on the different kinds of machines you can chose from, as well as other useful "toys" you may want to buy.

There are different kinds of juicers to chose from:

- Centrifugal force, where the pulp stays in the machine, like the Omega;
- Separator, where the pulp goes out one side and the juice the other, such as the Juice Man or the Moulinex;
- Masticating, which often does much more than juice, like the Champion;
- Triturator, which doesn't tear up the food, but crushes it, like the Green Power Machine or the Norwalk, which also does much more than juice.

I prefer a machine that does more rather than less, and there have been times when I just wanted to juice a few items. Pick the right one for your budget and space considerations.

Champion Juicer *(a masticating juicer):* Much more than a juicer, its strong suit is juicing fruits. (You can put the pulp through more than once for a foamy, textured juice.) This machine can also do sorbets, nut butters, pâtés, and seed or nut loafs.

Green Power Machine *(a triturator):* This is the green juicer (for wheat grass, as well as any green vegetable). It also makes pâtés, cookie dough, a raw pasta, nut or seed loafs, and bread sticks, as well as raw bread dough, sorbets, salsas, and sauces. See my book *Living With Green Power: A Gourmet Collection of Living Foods* for more recipes especially designed for this machine.

Blender: Excellent for sauces, salsa, soups, dips, and sorbet. This is a less expensive choice than the Vita-Mix—not as efficient, but certainly good enough for beginners. There is a bartender version that is more powerful than the drug store version— look for it in department stores or Home Club-type stores.

Vita-Mix: I recommend the Commercial Drink Machine model for two reasons: it has a clear blender top, so you can see what you are doing, and it has a high/low option, as well as a variable-speed dial. This model is more powerful and does a better job than the regular Vita-Mix. Its blades are designed to break up the toughest grain, nut, or seed. It is excellent for sauces, salsas, soups, dips, cookie dough, bread dough, smoothies, sorbet, and any blended food. There now is a separate blender top for doing grains and other dry ingredients. It has a specially designed blade, geared to handle dry blending better than the "wet" model.

Food processor: Small or large, these are handy tools for salsas, soups, sorbets, slaws, certain sauces, dips, pâtés, and for slicing and grating large amounts of foods. I personally enjoy the Oskar Sunbeam for small jobs and the Braun for larger ones.

Nut & seed grinder (also called a coffee bean grinder): This is mainly used for spices and seeds or nuts. (If soaked, nuts or seeds have to be sun dried or dehydrated to blend, otherwise they turn to mush.)

Excalibur dehydrator: For most people, a 9-tray model is needed. This size is the most versatile for making dehydrator breads, crackers, cookies, "baked" fruit or veggies, fruit leathers, dried fruits, puddings, and dried vegetables to be used as spices or garnishes—plus more. The trays can be added or taken out to allow for pie dishes or flat cracker/cookie trays as needed—modular spacing is an option you want in a dehydrator. Also, this dehydrator blows hot air across the food—not up from below, which heats the lowest tray most. The food on all the trays are equally dehydrated. Make sure to order the teflex sheets. They make dehydrating liquids a pleasure, and you can reuse these sheets over and over again.

Rival electric skillet: For warming casseroles, soups, sauces, dips, and desserts, this particular brand can be used on the warm setting, and, if watched carefully, can keep the food temperature below 105°F. Whether you chose the smaller or larger version of this skillet, this will revolutionize your kitchen as it did mine. I am now able to warm dishes without killing all the enzymes. As long as you can keep your finger in the dish without it becoming uncomfortable, the food is not too hot. To keep this machine happy, use non-scratch utensils. If well-maintained, you'll get years of use from this "tool."

Coffee warming plate: This electric appliance is traditionally used to keep coffee warm in those lovely glass coffee pots. The beauty of this tool is that it warms and doesn't heat rapidly. It will reach temperatures that could cook the food if not watched, but it provides a fun way to keep teas warm and a lovely way to warm up those porridges on cool mornings. As with any tool that heats, keep a careful eye on how hot the food is getting. The easiest guide is if the food is warm to the touch, it is warm enough. If the food gets too hot to touch, it is cooking; take it off the heat imme-diately, and serve. With this tool there is no thermostat, just an on and off switch. So your watchful eye (and fingers) will be needed to monitor the amount of heat.

Kitchen tools you'll appreciate

Chopping boards: Wooden ones are the best. Two are a good idea: one for the more fragrant spices like garlic and onions and the other for everything else.

Sharp knives: I enjoy Henckels, as well as Japanese varieties. Find at least two: a smaller blade for slicing and a larger knife for fine mincing. (The blade needs to rock from tip to handle for thorough mincing action.) My favorite knives are made from zirconia, a ceramic material that is harder than steel. You can order them from Kyrocera in San Diego, California (see page 135). These knives rarely have to be sharpened, and a cut from these knives creates less oxidation of your food.

Graters: Get at least two kinds, one that juliennes and one that does standard grat-ing. The Multi-slicer (less than $12 in some stores) is my favorite for the variety of things it does; the julienne cut it makes is the best I have found. Your other grater should do standard grates. I found a grater at Star Restaurant Supply (see page 135) that has six sides (functions) and is made in Switzerland. It stands on its own and can fine-grate, slice, coarse-grate, or "grate" citrus peel. I enjoy it because it doesn't scrape my fingers or knuckles.

Glass pie plates: Pyrex makes the best I have found for making puddings or mousse. It is a convenient form for seed or nut "cheeses" and sorbet or fruit pies, as well as a lovely serving form for chips and dips.

Cookie cutters: Not a must, but so much fun for making holiday treats. I have found great selections at restaurant supply stores, Japanese markets, and other kitchen equipment stores. Have fun picking out your favorites.

Peeler: A sharp peeler can help take off the wax from cucumbers or apples. Unless you have a wax deficiency, your body can't digest it—best to peel it off. Better yet, buy unwaxed fruits and vegetables. Kyrocera makes a ceramic version of this tool.

Wooden, glass, or stainless steel bowls: These materials are friendly to the foods you will be preparing. Plastic gives off a gas and should be used only when absolute-ly necessary.

Widemouthed/lidded glass jars: For soaking, germinating, sprouting, and fer-menting, glass is best. Widemouthed jars are easier to get ingredients in and out of, plus the lids make them easier to store in the refrigerator once the food has been rinsed or partially eaten.

Evolving the Alchemy of Designing a Living Food Menu or Dish

Recently I shared the recipes I had used in two years of workshops and TV shows with a friend who asked me, "Elysa, how did you learn to do this? Who influenced you or taught you how to not cook?"

I liked his questions and felt that you might also want to know how I learned to do all of this. When I first started eating this way, I didn't know what I was doing. If you would've asked me what I ate, I honestly couldn't have told you. I had a hit-and-miss approach. From one day to the next, I would eat what was in season, making up new dishes—new to me at least.

My digestion wasn't very good. The sour taste in my mouth, constant gas, and occasional constipation were all symptoms that gave me a clear message—do something different, please. The first step I took was to get my juicer out and start juicing again. I had juiced during my twenties, and I remembered how much better I had felt then. I started to feel better.

Shopping at the farmers' market, I would buy in-season, organic produce and create juices. *Food For Thought: Elysa's Private Recipe Collection*, my first recipe book, was a wide variety of juice recipes. It eventually was "translated" into *Living With Green Power: A Gourmet Collection of Living Food Recipes*, published by Alive Books in 1997. It fulfilled a dream I had to create a living foods recipe book with full color photographs.

People often ask me what juicer I recommend. The one I use most is the Moulinex for portability and ease of use while traveling. Recently, I was introduced to the Green Power Machine, and it does green juices by far the best. I have enjoyed wheat grass juice as well as the greens I can buy in any market: celery, lettuce, anise, bok choy, spinach, kale, to mention a few of my favorites. The Champion Juicer does a fine job of juicing fruit. And there are other juicers I have enjoyed. The point is, put your juicer on the counter, and use it, whichever one you like.

When you say raw or living foods to most people, they think salads. So did I. During my first year of eating raw and living foods, I was influenced by a man who was thrilled by eating just a head of lettuce, no dressing, nothing else, for dinner. That was enough for him. Not for me. I wanted more colors, more flavors, more tastes—more of a meal. I remember walking through the market, literally feeling dizzy and disoriented, not knowing what to buy. Changing any habits takes time and patience. It took me over a year to get comfortable knowing where to find food in the market—on the outer aisles, where the fruits and vegetables are usually kept.

So, how did I get from being dizzy to feeling comfortable making new food choices? Good question. The first book I read that helped me was Elizabeth Baker's *The UnCook Book*. In 1997, I had the privilege to meet her (still going strong at 85) and spend time at her home in Washington state. I told her about reading her books years ago and how she inspired me with this form of food preparation. I shared *Living with Green Power* with her, and she paid me one of the highest compliments I could have received when she looked at my recipe book, and said, "Elysa, the student has surpassed the teacher." I was humbled and flattered, and she continues to inspire me to this day.

I found a few other books that helped me (see pages 137), but I needed to meet people who ate this way and could show me how to fix some of these foods. Soaking was a strange concept for me. Fermenting foods was even stranger. So I started talking to other people who ate living foods and discovered that for most of them there was a transition period.

I had leapt in with both feet—and rebounded just as far (well, not quite). I had gone on a six-day cleansing fast in May of 1991, from a "healthy" Standard American Diet (SAD)—you know, chicken and fish, dairy and bottled juices—and went straight to a raw/living foods diet for six months. After the initial energy boost, I felt tired. I slept a lot. I needed time to heal systems that had been damaged for a long time by eating too much, eating too late, and eating combinations that didn't work for me.

After six months of eating cold, raw foods, winter set in, and I missed warmed food. Spicing became my next lesson for warming living foods. One of the first people who opened the door of spicing for me was Johnny Lynch. I call him the "Spice King" of living foods—he loves his spices. He appeared on many of my shows, sharing his style of spicing, blending, dehydrating, and combining foods in his own uniquely fresh and lively manner. I started paying more attention to how I felt after eating spicy foods—sometimes stimulated (too much at times), other times deliciously delighted.

Johnny helped me understand how to use grains: sprouting them and using them in salads, blending them into loafs, or even making desserts. I was especially delighted to learn how to use soaked raw grains for food dishes. Vitamin B is so important for nerve regeneration and mine were depleted, having lived in Los Angeles most of my life. The oxymoron of cooking foods to consume a vitamin that is destroyed by heating made no sense to me. Soaking, germinating, and sprouting the grains did make sense, so I started to take Johnny's recipes and play with them. They satisfied a need I had for grains and sweets, and warmed me up during a cold winter.

I had always been the person to make the salads for our family celebrations, so coming up with salad recipes was not new for me. What was new was finding ways to give the vegetables texture through slicing, dicing, and grating. It was about this time that I met Anthony and Deborah Boyar. Anthony had found a grater in Switzerland that he imports to the U.S., and I bought one from him. This Swiss grater is gentle on the hands and enhances the flavors of the vegetables by grating them with a fine double-grating action. The vegetables almost taste juiced instead of grated. The obvious benefit is that the fiber and the juice are both in the salad. I have since found a six-sided grater that costs less and does the job very well (see page 135).

Warming up foods can also be done in a dehydrator, and Deborah shared her dehydrated rye cracker recipe on one of my TV shows. It got me thinking of how I could create foods that were warm and crunchy. Textures and temperatures are important when you are changing habits. Deborah and I talked about our difficulties and joys in letting go of old habits of eating. I felt more supported to change what I was doing. Seeing how healthy Anthony looked after over 20 years on this kind of diet helped also.

Deborah is a fine example of a person who can enjoy the same meal day after day. You may be like her. Less is more. You might find one recipe and stick with it for months. Do it. Having been raised gourmet Jewish, I tend to enjoy more variety, but I can definitely relate to eating simply.

Around the same time, I met another creative couple who have been enjoying living foods for a while—Jamey Dina and Kim Sproul. Their experience with the Excalibur Dehydrator was an inspiration for me. They sold me my first dehydrator, as well as my second one. My dehydrator has been one of my most frequently used kitchen machines. I have come up with recipes that both surprised and delighted me. For example, the pecan mousse—who would have thought that a nut could taste fluffy?

Jamey and Kim also introduced me to a spice called Tomato Delight, made in Texas, that makes salad dressings and squash dishes so tasty. (Try the "Squabetti" on page 80 with that sprinkled on top.) There is a new spice that has taken over the legacy Marianna Fry, the originator of Tomato Delight, created. Phyllis Avery makes Tomato

Tornado and other organic, dehydrated powdered spices that are delightful to use (see page 133). Before knowing Jamie and Kim, I had never heard of a grain called kamut, because it is only found in health food stores (and not all of them). I have not included any of those recipes here in this book, but you might want to experiment with this unusual, high-protein grain. Kim and Jamey have developed recipes using this grain in an amazing array of dishes. As guests on my show, they presented recipes from simple to sublime, from pizza to pâtés. *Food For Thought: Elysa's Private Recipe Collection* includes these and other recipes from my special TV show guests. They also have their own recipe book (see page 134 for ordering information).

After a few months of experimenting with my dehydrator at 115°F-120°F, Johnny Lynch informed me that amino acids are destroyed at around 108°F, so I lowered it to 105°F. I discovered that dehydrating has an alchemy all of its own. Drying changes the flavors of many different kinds of food, which you too can experiment with.

In September, 1993, Adia, an amazing, beautiful, 6'2" yogini appeared on my show and shared the art of texturizing germinated (soaked) nuts and vegetables together, as well as warming with sunshine—inspiring the celebration loaf and sauce recipe in this book. So even if I didn't have a dehydrator, I could use my porch, a window in my home, or even use my car if I was traveling.

I used to stop by Kevin's (and Adia's) restaurant, now sadly closed, and loved relating my latest finds, while enjoying Kevin and Adia's wonderful food. Also a master at spicing, Adia shared with me how her own tastes have simplified over time. I enjoyed learning how they came to a simpler style, eating one food for a meal—known as "mono" eating.

Everyone finds the best approach for themselves. That is what I am hoping to inspire you to do also. Find your own way into this style of eating—there's no rush. Let it evolve naturally.

Two weeks after the big Los Angeles earthquake, January 17, 1991, I traveled to Santa Cruz in northern California to be a guest lecturer. There I became acquainted with Beverly Peterson at a Living Foods Specialist Training Workshop organized by Steve Hurwitz. Beverly jumped right in and helped me prepare food for fifteen people without a second thought. Both of these talented people shared ideas and approaches. Marinating vegetables intrigued me about Steve's approach. For example, "pickles" can be easily made by marinating cucumbers in fresh dill weed, crushed dill seed, lemon juice, and soy sauce, or Bragg Liquid Aminos. I also enjoy adding Annie's Shiitake Vinaigrette Dressing for another flavor. Many vegetables can be "warmed" with this kind of spicing/soaking.

Beverly is the quintessential gourmet chef. We spent months preparing and expanding each other's definition of what a living food artist can do. Her flair for designing and combining foods to make a meal contributed greatly to this book. As I taught her, she shared with me—an exchange took place that expanded both of us. I would call her with recipes, and she'd share hers with me. Beverly reminded me that when food looks good, we enjoy our meal more—design and decorate each dish you serve, even if it is only for yourself. You deserve to eat lovely food too.

In November, 1993, I attended a demonstration workshop at the American Living Foods Institute (ALFI), where I met Edwin Douglas and Lynn Orion. They opened yet another door of the alchemy of living foods: warming with an electric skillet. They served a gently warmed curry entree and offered a training program for participants to learn how to prepare meals in the ALFI fashion. Ed had developed the warming concept into a science and clearly enjoyed sharing this art with others. This experience influenced me to further develop and enhance the warming concept.

I went home and spent six months embellishing on this approach, warming foods using the Rival skillet. With delight, I developed recipes from sixteen countries that I incorporated into workshops called "Eating in the Raw Around the World"—soon to be written into a series of recipe books.

I later spent some time at the Institute and helped them promote their approach to the living food lifestyle. What impressed me about the ALFI approach was the simplicity of the recipes. As you read this book, enjoy making the food simply. Each food does have its own wonderful taste, and you can enjoy exploring and experiencing as I have done, by simplifying.

It is in doing that we learn. I learned from these friends, as well as other individuals, that living foods gives me more energy. Coming from an American-Jewish-Beverly Hills-gourmet style of life, I look for texture, taste, and temperature to tempt my taste buds. When I want to eat a food I used to "enjoy," I look for a more nutritious substitute most of the time. I am still learning how to give up some of my food addictions. I still find sugar (especially honey) appealing. But as I listen to Nancy Appleton, who wrote *Lick The Sugar Habit* (and has appeared on my show in a segment with the same title), I am reminded to find more nutritious sources of sugar. One can combine fruits with nuts to slow the assimilation of fruit sugar into the system. Once the nuts or seeds are soaked, they change chemical composition—they transmute—and then they are much easier to digest with fruit. Understanding what happens during the soaking and germinating process helps folks who follow strict food combining practices relax and enjoy nuts, seeds, and fruits together (and enjoy another breakfast choice).

I have stopped judging myself if I eat something and I don't feel well afterwards. Learning takes time. I am giving myself the gift of time. Do the same for yourself. Don't make this a religion or a reason to feel bad if you eat differently. We are all evolving into better people. Patience is the first "food for thought" we need to indulge in regularly. I lived with a person who constantly judged me for what I ate, accused me of tempting him to sin. You won't go to hell for eating anything. Notice when you eat foods and feel better. Keep on looking and experimenting for yourself. You'll find what is best for you.

The winter of 1994-95 I had the opportunity to prepare food for Dr. Gabriel Cousens at his Tree of Life Rejuvenation Center in Patagonia, Arizona. I helped organize their kitchen. What a delight to pick fresh produce from an organic garden for the meals we created daily. Here I had a chance to put to practice what I had been learning for the last four years. Breakfasts were fruit and nut/seed sauces. By warming the food with ginger, I learned more about applying Indian principles of how foods strengthen or weaken different constitutions, or body types: vata, pitta, kapha.

With my partner, Darrell, I did two main meals a day for between ten and twenty people, on average. I warmed using all my learned and created skills: hot water for warmed cereals; the sun for sun teas; the skillet for soups, sauces, grain casseroles, and vegetable stews; the dehydrator for breads, pastries, puddings and desserts that delighted everyone; employing an Ayurvedic approach by using spices like cumin and ginger that warm the body and also strengthen digestion.

If I didn't have an ingredient, I would improvise or change the recipe. Each day was a delight and a challenge to feed people a balanced diet that varied. The point was that the food was good for them, looked good, and tasted delicious.

Change takes time and getting used to some of the practices, like soaking or sprouting, will be less bothersome once you get in a rhythm with it. The importance of soaking and sprouting is that you are creating a living food, one that will or could sprout. It's like creating a miniature garden in your kitchen. Soaking dissolves enzymes that inhibit digestion, making the food easier to digest. Almonds, for example, once soaked are much easier to digest. The enzyme lipase, which digests fats, is contained in the nut and made easier to assimilate once it has been soaked and germinated.

Let this book inspire you to taste, to create, to become as healthy as you can. Write me and let me know about your discoveries.

Recipe Information

I have included several kinds of information on some of the recipe pages for your assistance.

Ingredients and Ingredient Options

Always buy in season. If the food listed is not in season, substitute one that is. It will taste better and offer you more nutrients. Often I am tempted to buy out of season. Every time I do, I am disappointed; it just doesn't taste as good. Out-of-season foods are often imported. You may also be getting more pesticides from foods grown in countries that use pesticides that have been banned in this country.

Make sure to spice to your own taste. I did not put exact spicing amounts for this reason. You may want more or less. Always use less and add after tasting. The trickiest recipes are those intended for the dehydrator. The flavors concentrate and generally get stronger after dehydration.

Most of these recipes can be made with more than one food. *Experiment with what you have in your refrigerator, garden, or local markets.*

Machine Options

Preparation can often be done more than one way or with more than one machine. Use what you have until you are comfortable expanding. Then buy the next or newer machine. Talk to someone who owns one before you buy it. Their experience can add to yours.

The differences among machines is usually the texture they create. A blender will not be as powerful as a Vita-Mix, but it will do the job if allowed to blend longer or at a higher speed.

Yield: How many servings or cups you will get

The yield will vary slightly with the size of the produce and how you measure. I am not a careful measurer, so you might have variations in the yields. Also, a serving size can vary. I have tried to be as uniform as possible; be flexible.

Preparation Time

Preparation time includes time for soaking, preparing, freezing, and dehydrating, if applicable.

Soaking time can vary and does from recipe book to book, depending on who you read. On average, between 8 to 24 hours is sufficient for most nuts and seeds. Another rule of thumb is to soak what you will use for the next day. I used to store soaked nuts and seeds for days or weeks, only to be disappointed in their diminished taste. If they didn't keep, I'd end up tossing them out.

Sprouting time takes longer for some of the grains. However, I have tried to keep this at a minimum. The longest time I have experimented with is 24 hours for almonds. For most other kinds of nuts or seeds, between 8 to 12 hours is sufficient. It may be different for you to have to think about what you will or might eat tomorrow and prepare it by soaking. Keep some soaked nuts or seeds on hand, so you are prepared, just in case. Once you get used to soaking, it will be a simple process for you to soak and rinse. Use what you need.

Dehydrating time can also vary depending on where you live, so check your first couple of batches. In Arizona it took much less time than in California at the beach. Decide how dry you want your food or how long you want to leave it in the dehydrator.

To help make this menu plan work more easily for you, I am including what to do for the next day's menu in the recipe sections called *"Preparations for the next meal."* If you plan to make a different meal than the one listed in the menu plan, look for those directions in the recipe you're substituting; they might require a day or two of planning. You can make most of these meals with simple soaking, but the sprouted grains and almond "yogurt" each take two days, one to soak and one to sprout or ferment.

Make Your Meals a Memorable Experience

Presentation is so much a part of the pleasure of any meal time. We start to eat with our eyes, then our memories of the food kick in, and we start to salivate and enjoy the thought of eating a dish, remembering how good the last one tasted. Putting it into our mouth is only a part of the satisfaction of any meal. So with any meal you choose to prepare, have fun "playing" with your food. Create a plate that your eyes can feast on first. Using a colorful plate or a decorated dish can enhance a presentation. I have found lovely dishes and bowls to serve my meals in; garage sales are great places to go to find just that special dish. Garnish your meal with a colorful food: fruit, vegetable, or spice. (Mint or parsley go with almost every dish.) Using cookie cutters, molds, just a ring of fruit, or decorating with a sprig of green around a bowl dresses even the most ordinary meal. And it only takes a moment to "dress up."

Eat in settings that are calm, cheerful, and bright. I put Christmas lights in my kitchen, as well as candles on the dining room table. On cloudy mornings, a bright, cheery kitchen can make coming to eat a treat.

Eating in season is always preferred. I know I look forward to the first fresh corn, the first fresh white peach, or the first persimmon that gets really ripe each year. The food tastes best and the nutrients are primed for that food being ripe in that season. Most foods grown out of the country are out of season. We pay a dear price for them, not only in cost, but in the pesticides used on them, loss of flavor, and lack of nutrients. I can't tell you how many times I have been disappointed in the melons and tomatoes I've tasted that were grown out of season. I have decided to wait. You might also. So, when the recipe calls for corn, and it is not corn season, wait—eat other foods that are in season. Salsa can be made without tomatoes, for example. Make a cilantro salsa, salsa "verde," instead. Salsa is a presentation style, not a particular recipe with ingredients that have to be strictly adhered to.

Which is also to say, please let the process of making these recipes be a creative one for you. If there is an ingredient you don't like, don't use it. If you want to substitute an ingredient for one you prefer, or one you have on hand, be playful and enjoy the process of creating new recipes for yourself. My intention is to inspire you, not to bind you to any hard or fast rules here. In considering what you should have on hand, you'll have more options if you have nuts or seeds already soaking. Because living foods cuisine takes a bit more thoughtfulness on your part, having ingredients presoaked will allow you more choices for your meal that day.

Let's Go Shopping

Buying organic is the first suggestion, but you've heard me say that already. It is still the most healthful rule of thumb when buying any kind of food.

Knowing what to have on hand makes menu planning more fun and less annoying; you won't be missing one ingredient. Sometimes, however, that is exactly how new recipes are born, when that's all you have on hand.

Storing the staples—nuts, seeds, beans, and grains—in glass helps the foods stay fresh longer. Keeping them in a dark, cool place enhances their shelf life even further.

Here are some simple suggestions of spices and foods to keep your pantry stocked with so you can make meals in minutes:

Spices:

__ allspice

__ basil

__ caraway seeds

__ cayenne

__ cinnamon

__ cilantro

__ cumin

__ dill

__ garlic (fresh cloves or granulated)

__ ginger (fresh root is best)

__ Italian spice blend

__ lemon (fresh and the peel)

__ Mexican spice blend

__ nutmeg (grated whole seed is tastiest fresh)

__ onion (flakes or Onion Magic)

__ parsley (fresh or dried)

__ poultry spice

__ Celtic salt (see the glossary on page 133)

__ turmeric

__ vanilla (nonalcoholic extract, or, better yet, the fresh bean)

__ Bragg Liquid Aminos and/or a soy seasoning

Salts and Salt Substitutes:

__ miso (a fermented soybean paste useful for soup broth; keep all miso refrigerated)

__ soy sauce

__ Bragg Liquid Aminos (a nonfermented soy-based seasoning liquid with a flavor similar to soy sauce)

__ Dr. Bronner's Minerals (a soy-vegetable combination

__ Dr. Jensen's Quick Sip (a soy-vegetable combination)

__ gomasio (sesame salt made from toasted sesame seeds and salt)

__ Vege-Sal (salt and other vegetable spice)

__ Mrs. Dash's Salt-Free Seasoning Blends (available in different flavors)

__ Spike with vegetable seasonings (has a salt-free version)

__ Celtic salt (see the glossary on page 133)

Seeds:

__ flax

__ sesame

__ sunflower

__ pumpkin

Nuts:

__ almonds

__ cashews

__ hazelnuts (filberts)

__ pecans

__ pine nuts

__ walnuts

Dried Fruits:

__ apricots (Turkish are my favorites)

__ currants

__ dates

__ mango

__ papaya

__ pineapple

__ peaches

__ raisins

__ your favorites

Grains:

__ barley

__ oats

__ wheat

__ rye

__ kamut

Beans:

__ aduki

__ lentils

__ mung

Fresh Fruits in Season:

__ bananas

__ apples

__ oranges

__ avocados

__ tomatoes (dried and fresh)

__ your favorites

Sea vegetables:

__ nori sheets

__ dulse

__ kelp

Fresh vegetables:

__ baby greens

__ larger leafy greens (romaine, red leaf, butter leaf, red oak, or whatever organic greens you can find)

__ carrots

__ celery

__ cucumber

__ cabbage

__ kale

__ broccoli

__ bell peppers

Sprouts:

__ alfalfa

__ clover

__ sunflower

I find when I have fresh food on hand, I eat more fresh food. Whatever is losing its freshness I can juice, dehydrate, or freeze. Keeping soaked nuts, seeds, beans, and grains readily available gives me more options for recipes and snacks.

Don't go out and buy everything on this list all at once. First, clear white sugar, white salt, white flour, and processed items out of your kitchen to make room for the "good" stuff. Get a few items from each category. Let it be an adventure to create a new kitchen with better food choices in it for you and your family. Find farmers' markets and stores that you enjoy shopping in, and let this be a pleasure.

Menu for 7 days

Day 1

Breakfast: Golden Applesauce

Lunch: Creamy Cashew Soup with Bush Broccoli Salad & Blushing Vinaigrette Dressing

Dinner: Stuffed Peppers & Creamy Thousand Island Dressing
with A Grate Salad & Better Beet Dressing

Dessert: Almond Cookies

Snack: A Dressed Naked Veggie Platter

Drink: Blushing Garden Juice

Day 2

Breakfast: Brainy Breakfast Chowder

Lunch: Sunned Patty with Lightly Lemoned Coleslaw

Dinner: "Squabetti" Squash with Simply Italian Salad & Basic Italian Dressing

Dessert: Rainbow Sorbet

Snack: Ricotta "Cheese" Spread with Veggie "Chips"

Drink: "Sun" Teas

Day 3

Breakfast: Date with an Oat Groat

Lunch: Celebration Loaf with Darrell's Cilantro Special Salad

Dinner: Tostada with Salsa & Guacamole

Dessert: Pecan Mousse

Snack: Mexi-Flax Crisps

Drink: Lean Green Juice

Day 4

Breakfast: Scrambled Corn with Veggie "Chips" & Salsa "Verde"
Lunch: Eggplant "Pizza" with Creamy Spinach Soup
Dinner: Tabouli with Royal Tahini Dip
Dessert: Strawberry Cream Pie
Snack: Rye Bread Sticks with Avocado Sauce
Drink: A Berry Delicious Drink

Day 5

Breakfast: Cherie's Sprouted Cereal for Champions
Lunch: Cauliflower Casserole with Autumn Salad & Green Goddess Dressing
Dinner: "Asparagusto" Soup with Orange U Glad It's Salad? & Tangy Orange Dressing
Dessert: Date Nut Torte
Snack: Ah Nuts (a cucumber and nut treat)
Drink: Pineapple Delight

Day 6

Breakfast: Digest'aid' Diva's Drink
Lunch: Pecan Pâté with Veggie "Chips"
Dinner: Barley Warmed Casserole with Radishly Green Salad & Creamy Italian Dressing
Dessert: "Unbaked" Apple
Snack: A Date with a Sweetie
Drink: Orange You Glad We've Got Omega-3 Oils Blend?

Day 7

Breakfast: Glorious Garden Hi-Pro "Fundue" with Veggie "Chips"
Lunch: Broccoli Soup with Golden Spinach Salad & Lemon Dill Dressing
Dinner: Unbaked Beans with Greens
Dessert: Hawaiian Treats
Snack: Sunny Seed "Cheese" Dip with Jicama
Drink: Banini Shake

Breakfast Choices

Day 1—Golden Applesauce

A deliciously warmed applesauce, with fruit chips to dip into on a cool morning.

Apples, raisins, Calimyrna figs, cinnamon, and nutmeg, with a choice of apple, pear, apricot, peach, or plum chips.

Day 2—Brainy Breakfast Chowder

Wake up to a brain-enhancing breakfast, rich in omega-3 essential fatty acids and your vitamins and minerals in a bowl.

Zinc-rich pumpkin and flax seeds with carrot juice and fresh vegetables blended and spiced to perfection naturally with avocado, parsley, celery, and cucumber.

Day 3—Date with an Oat Groat

A warmed, cinnamon-spiced, date-sweetened, full-bodied oat porridge.

Oat groats, dates, cinnamon, raisins, almond "milk."

Day 4—Scrambled Corn with Veggie "Chips" & Salsa "Verde"

A creamy scrambled corn served with a rainbow of vegetable "chips" and salsa "verde."

Fresh corn off the cob, olive oil, cumin, Celtic salt, dulse and/or kelp;

Veggie "chips": jicama, cabbage, squash, carrots, red bell pepper, cilantro;

Salsa: cilantro, green onions, celery, garlic, lime.

Day 5—Cherie's Sprouted Cereal for Champions

A sprouted multi-grain morning cereal with a creamy banana topping, a wake-up call rich in vitamin B—nerve food to nourish and calm your nerves.

Rye, wheat or kamut, buckwheat groats, millet, sprouting barley;

Banana "milk" with vanilla beans and sunflower seeds.

Day 6 —Digest'aid' Diva's Drink

Blended whole fruits, warmed to thrill your mouth and tummy on cool mornings with just the right blend of enzymes, chlorophyll, and essential fatty acids to make your morning start out brightly.

Pineapple, papaya, strawberries, banana, alfalfa or clover sprouts, flax seeds, plus a "green powder" (Barley Green, Pure Synergy, or The Ultimate Meal, etc.), fresh gingerroot.

Day 7—Glorious Garden Hi-Pro "Fundue" with Veggie "Chips"

Blended almond "yogurt" with a high-protein choice of vegetables for dipping and dunking.

"Fundue": almond "yogurt," mustard;

Veggie "chips": broccoli flowers and stalks, celery, cabbage, yams, bell peppers, lettuce.

A word about breakfast

These breakfast menus are intended as choices, inspiration for you to see that there are simple and healthful ways to start your day. Please know that you can also make the choice to pick up an apple or a bell pepper, just as it is, and start out your day with a single simple food, uncut, unprocessed, and unadulterated. Whether your system needs fruits, vegetables, or grains, any of these are choices for you in the morning.

Some mornings I don't want to chew, so I go to the blender, throw in whole foods, and come up with a meal in a glass. Whether it is primarily fruit, vegetables, or a combination of both that my body can handle, it's what I call a "no brainer"—no complicated thinking involved, just toss and blend. Other days I want my breakfast to crunch, so I create a meal to munch on that could be as simple as a date with an apple or a tomato with a stalk of celery. Melons are best eaten alone. A wonderfully colorful breakfast is a combination of three types of melons, such as honeydew, cantaloupe, and watermelon.

If it is particularly cold and I want to enjoy a whole food, I can put it in warm water to take the chill off. Or I can warm up the serving bowls by putting them into hot water. Starting off the morning with a warm cup of tea, or even warm water with a slice of gingerroot and lemon juice, can warm the coldest tummy.

Fruit and vegetable "chips" warm up quickly when placed in a warm oven or in a warm bowl. It can take as little as two to five minutes to take the chill out and warm up your breakfast. Leave the oven on low (less than 200°F), or turn it on, let it warm up, turn it off, and put the food in, leaving the door opened a bit to keep it from "cooking."

I have left a cored apple in the dehydrator overnight only to find it "baked" by morning (see page 108 in the dessert section). You might prefer that for breakfast. The pecan mousse on page 102 is another of my favorites for breakfast. Don't let the categories limit you as to the time of day they are served. You might want soup or salad for breakfast and a fruit dish for dinner—let your body tell you what it would enjoy for that meal.

Some days juice is enough, with one of my favorite blended "green potions," like Pure Synergy or Barley Green. Green powder just stirred into plain, filtered water can set my day going fine. What I have on hand or can buy in season, fresh and organic, is usually my first choice. However, the weather can condition my mood, whether or not I ate late the night before (which I am doing less and less of these days), or whether I have company for that meal—all of these play into what I choose to prepare.

Golden Applesauce

Day 1

Yield: 2 servings

15 minutes to prepare

A deliciously warmed applesauce with fruit "chips" to dip into on a cool morning.

**¼ to ½ cup raisins
3 apples
2 to 4 Calimyrna figs (or any nonsulfured fig)
Cinnamon
Fresh nutmeg
Gingerroot (optional)
Fruit "chips": apple, pear, apricot, peach, or plums**

**Optional ingredients:
Fresh fruit in season, walnuts, pecans, celery, lettuce, or
hemp seed oil**

1. Put the raisins in a blender with about ½ cup of water (enough to enable you to blend them), and blend to a sauce-like consistency. Add the apples and figs, and blend to the desired consistency.

2. Spice with cinnamon, fresh nutmeg, and/or ginger to taste.

3. If you want the sauce to be warm, either use hot water when you blend or place the sauce in a saucepan and warm it over a very low flame for a very short time. Use your finger to test the temperature. If it gets too warm, turn off heat.

4. Serve in a lovely bowl surrounded by sliced fruit "chips."

Ingredient Options: Currants or cranberries can be used for a more tart apple-sauce. You could use dates instead of raisins and figs. With the right date, this can taste almost like caramel applesauce. For some, adding nuts and/or greens tempers the fruit sugar and makes it easier to eat without the sugar highs and lows. Just line the bowl with lettuce leaves or shredded lettuce, and put the sauce on top, sprinkled with crushed walnuts or pecans. Celery can be added for crunch with the fruit "chips," making this like a Waldorf salad without the mayonnaise. To make a creamier sauce, add a bit of hemp oil to the blender (up to ½ teaspoon) before blending. Be careful of how much gingerroot you add; it tastes hot and can dominate the flavor. Use a small slice without the skin, and add it a little at a time. You can always add more; taking it out is the challenge.

Machine Options: A regular blender will do, although a Vita-Mix does it quicker and will warm up the sauce by blending it longer. The Champion or Green Power machines can also make applesauce. If you use the Champion, take out all the screens, and let the food drop into a bowl. The Green Power Machine works best with the open blank. If a creamier sauce is desired, use the closed blank.

Warming Options: You can use a Vita-Mix, saucepan, electric warming/hot plate, or dehydrator (between 4 to 6 hours at 105°F). When I use the dehydrator, I prepare this dish the night before. Then I wake up to a warmed, flavor-enhanced, saucy breakfast.

Next-Day Preparation for the Brainy Breakfast Chowder:

Soak ½ cup flax seeds in a glass container, and soak 2 to 4 teaspoons pumpkin seeds in a separate glass container.

Brainy Breakfast Chowder

Day 2

Yield: 2 servings

8 to 12 hours to soak
10 minutes to prepare

Zinc-rich pumpkin and flax seeds with carrot juice and fresh vegetables blended and spiced to perfection naturally.

**¼ cup pumpkin seeds
2 teaspoons flax seeds
2 to 3 cups carrot juice
1 avocado
¼ to ½ cup parsley
1 to 2 celery stalks
1 small unwaxed cucumber**

**Optional ingredients:
Corn, tomatoes, yams, romaine lettuce, red leaf lettuce**

1. Soak the pumpkin seeds overnight; rinse and drain. Soak the flax seeds overnight. The flax seeds do not need to be rinsed.

2. In a Vita-Mix or blender, puree all the ingredients, adding about 1 to 2 cups warm or cool water to thin the "broth" to the desired consistency and achieve the desired temperature.

3. If you would like a chunky chowder, choose from the optional ingredients. Mince them to the desired size, and add to the "broth" to make into a chowder.

Scrambled Corn with Veggie "Chips," pages 36-37, and Salsa, page 84

Ingredient Options: Vegetables are just as tasty in the morning as fruit. The greens add chlorophyll and many valuable vitamins and minerals. Corn, yams, and tomatoes add a sweet flavor, whereas lettuce adds greens to the meal.

Machine Options: A food processor with an "S" blade can be used, but it will make a much crunchier "broth." A Vita-Mix makes the creamiest "broth," but the pumpkin seeds (so rich in zinc) blend easily enough even in a regular blender.

Warming Options: You can use warm water or a Vita-Mix. (The longer you blend the warmer it gets.) You can also take the vegetables out of the refrigerator the night before so they are not as cold to begin with.

Next-Day Preparation for the Oat Groat Cereal:
Soak separately 1 cup of oat groats and ¼ cup of almonds. You can choose to soak the pitted dates or any of the dried fruit, if you prefer a softer, easier-to-chew fruit.

Notes

Cherie's Sprouted Cereal for Champions, pages 38-39, and A Berry Delicious Drink, page 129

Date with an Oat Groat

Day 3

Yield: 2 servings

12 to 24 hours to soak
10 minutes to prepare

A warmed, cinnamon-spiced, date-sweetened, full-bodied oat porridge.

1 cup oat groats (a groat is the whole oat)
¼ cup soaked almonds
4 to 6 pitted soaked dates
1 to 2 cups hot water
Cinnamon
Raisins

Optional ingredients:
Fresh berries, currants, black mission figs, Turkish dried
apricots, pearled barley, bananas

1. Soak the oat groats for 4 to 6 hours; drain. Soak the almonds for 12 to 24 hours; rinse.

2. Soak the pitted dates for 30 minutes.

3. In a Vita-Mix or blender, puree the oat groats and 2 to 4 dates, depending on how sweet you like your porridge. Thin to the desired consistency with hot water.

4. In a Vita-Mix or blender, make an almond "milk" by blending the soaked, rinsed almonds in warm or cool water with 2 to 4 more of the dates. For a creamer "milk," add a banana. Thin or thicken with water to achieve the desired consistency; strain, if desired, before serving.

5. Serve the groats in a cup or bowl, sprinkled with cinnamon and raisins. Top with almond milk.

Ingredient Options: You can use the soaking water to help sweeten this cereal without adding other sweeteners. Raisins, currants, or black mission figs could be substituted for the dates. A real treat is Turkish dried apricots. (I have only found these in quality health food stores, but they are worth the time and extra expense.) Barley could be substituted for the oats; it provides a different flavor and is also tasty. The almond milk can be made thin or thick depending on the amount of water you use and whether or not a banana is added. The dates sweeten the "milk," so decide how sweet you would enjoy it on your cereal. Dried fruits are easier to chew if they are pre-soaked in warm water. Make sure they are not dried in sulfur-dioxide; a dull color usually indicates a natural drying process.

You can also use sprouting oat groats which will take longer to sprout. Soak them for 12 hours. They will take 12 to 24 hours more to sprout. See page 136 for suppliers.

Machine Options: A food processor is possible, fitted with an "S" blade, but it will make a much crunchier porridge. A regular blender does just fine for this recipe. I like a crunchier oat cereal, but I certainly have made this in a Vita-Mix, as well, especially if I am making larger amounts or I want to use the machine to warm the food or "milk."

Warming Options: Process longer in a Vita-Mix, or use warm/hot water to blend with. You can also use a saucepan or a hot/warming plate, but watch carefully so they do not "cook" your meal.

Next-Day Preparation for Scrambled Corn:

Blend the salsa ingredients if you want the flavors to "meld" for a day; otherwise, make the salsa fresh the day you want to eat it.

Day-5 Preparation for Cherie's Sprouted Cereal:

Start soaking the rye, wheat or kamut, buckwheat groats, millet, and sprouting barley (2 cups in all) to give them time to expand.

Scrambled Corn with Veggie "Chips" and Salsa "Verde"

Day 4

Yield: 2 to 4 servings

15 minutes to prepare

A creamy scrambled corn served with a rainbow of vegetable "chips" and salsa "verde."

2 ears corn per person, kernels removed
1 to 2 tablespoons olive oil
½ to 1 teaspoon cumin
½ to 1 teaspoon turmeric
¼ to ½ teaspoon Celtic salt (optional)
Dulse or kelp "flakes"

Salsa "Verde":
1 cup cilantro (stalks, leaves, and all)
2 to 4 green onions (scallions)
2 stalks celery
¼ small unwaxed cucumber
1 to 2 cloves fresh garlic
2 to 4 tomatillos (optional)
½ chayote squash (optional)
1 to 2 limes
1 avocado, sliced

Veggie "Chips":
Sliced jicama, carrot, cucumber, squash, celery, red or green cabbage, red and/or yellow bell pepper, or any vegetable in season

1. In a food processor fitted with an "S" blade, pulse the corn kernels until creamed; keep them chunky, the consistency of scrambled eggs—not too smooth.

2. Set an electric skillet to a low or warm setting. Warm the oil, cumin, turmeric, and Celtic salt (if using), then add the processed corn kernels, and heat until just warm throughout. Spice with dulse and/or kelp to taste.

3. To make the salsa verde, place all of the salsa ingredients in a blender or a food processor fitted with an "S" blade and pulse, keeping the mixture chunky and spicing with lime juice and/or jalapeño peppers to taste.

4. Serve the corn warm with avocado slices, salsa, and fresh veggie "chips" on each plate, arranged decoratively.

Ingredient Options: If corn is not in season, the salsa and "chips" can be served with avocados on the "half shell" by cutting an avocado in half, filling it with salsa, and serving the veggie "chips" arranged colorfully on the plate. Tomato salsa is also an option to serve with this dish. Tomatillos look like small green tomatoes wrapped in a parchment covering. They are usually sold in markets that have Hispanic customers. Their flavor is more bitter than a tomato and is truly unique. They can be eaten alone or in a salsa or soup. Tomatillos have a slightly "waxy" coating which is natural for this food. I have not been able to wash it off, so don't despair if you can't either.

Machine Options: A food processor fitted with an "S" blade will make a much crunchier salsa than a blender. I have made it in a Vita-Mix as well, especially if I am making larger amounts.

Warming Options: Using an electric skillet set on low is my favorite way to warm this dish. You can also use a skillet warmed on a hot plate or a very low flame. Warm the skillet and then remove from the heat source.

Next-Day Preparation for Cherie's Sprouted Cereal:

Rinse the grains and let sprout on the counter for the day, putting them in the refrigerator for the evening after an evening rinse. Soak the sunflower seeds in the evening for the next day's "milk," plus any dried fruit you wish to eat with your cereal.

Cherie's Sprouted Cereal for Champions

Day 5

Yield: 2 servings

2 days to soak and sprout
10 minutes to prepare

A sprouted multi-grain morning cereal with a creamy banana topping.

2 cups total of the following dry grains: rye, wheat or kamut, buckwheat groats, millet, sprouting barley

Optional ingredients:
Quinoa, pearled barley, triticale, or other grains that will sprout; soaked dried fruit, or fresh fruit in season

1 to 2 bananas
¼ cup soaked sunflower seeds
1 inch fresh vanilla bean

1. Two evenings prior to eating, soak and rinse the grains. Let them sprout for a day, then rinse and place in the refrigerator until morning.

2. The day before eating, soak the sunflower seeds, then rinse and remove the hulls.

3. If using dried fruit, soak in warm water (100°F or so, slightly warmer than body temperature) for a short while (5 to 10 minutes), then mince to bite size.

4. To make sunflower milk on the day of the meal, mix one or two bananas, the sprouted, rinsed sunflower seeds, and the fresh vanilla bean in a Vita-Mix or blender, thinning with warm or cool water to the desired consistency and temperature.

5. Serve the sprouted grain with the warmed "milk" and minced, soaked dried fruit.

Ingredient Options: There are many grains that will sprout; choose your favorites. Quinoa will sprout by soaking for only a few hours and can easily be added to this cereal mix. If you are adding this protein-rich grain, do so on the second day of preparation for the meal, not on the first. The "milk" can be made with bananas alone, or the sunflower seeds can be blended with dried fruit of your choice.

Machine Options: A regular blender does just fine for this recipe. I have made this in a Vita-Mix as well, especially if I am making larger amounts or I want to warm it.

Warming Options: The "milk" and/or the cereal can be blended in a Vita-Mix to warm. A skillet or a warming (hot) plate can also be used. Ginger also warms the system when a fresh slice is blended into the "milk."

Next-Day Preparation for Digest'aid' Diva's Drink:

Soak ¼ cup flax seeds and ½ cup raisins for easier blending, if desired.

Day-7 Preparation for Almond "Yogurt":

Soak 3 cups of almonds.

Digest'aid' Diva's Drink

Day 6

Yield: 2 servings

2 to 4 hours to soak
10 minutes to prepare

Blended whole fruits, warmed to thrill your mouth and tummy on cool mornings with just the right blend of enzymes, chlorophyll, and essential fatty acids to make your morning start out brightly.

3 tablespoons flax seeds
½ cup organic raisins
¼ pineapple, skinned and cut into chunks
½ papaya, skinned, seeded, and cut into chunks
1 to 2 bananas, cut into chunks
1 cup hot water (optional)

1. Soak the flax seeds for 2 to 4 hours; drain. Soak the raisins for 20 minutes, drain, and save the soaking liquid.

2. In a blender, process all the ingredients together using the soaking water from the raisins and the flax seeds. Add the cut-up fruit gradually, pouring in about 1 cup hot water to warm the drink, if desired, or thin it to the desired consistency.

3. If serving warm, pour the drink into a warmed mug, or serve cool or at room temperature in a fancy glass.

Ingredient Options: One of the delights of this drink is that you can "chew" it rather than just chug it down. This is a much better way to enhance the digestion of this "meal in a glass." Pineapple and papaya have special digestive enzymes called bromelain and papain, respectively, which help to digest protein and are useful for reducing swelling in the body from an accident or surgery.

The soaking water can be used as a subtle way to sweeten this drink. Currants or black mission figs could be substituted for the raisins. You can blend a peeled orange into this drink for more fiber and a sweeter flavor. In the warmer months, you will probably prefer to make this with cool water. For more protein, add soaked almonds to this drink.

Machine Options: A regular blender does just fine for this recipe. Add the seeds first with the raisin soaking water. Begin by making a thick, smooth paste, then add the rest of the ingredients, thinning with water and/or thickening with more bananas.

Next-Day Preparation for Almond "Yogurt":

Blanch the skins off soaked, rinsed almonds by pouring very hot water over them, counting to 30, pouring it off, immediately pouring cool water over them, and then peeling off the skins right after rinsing. You can also use your finger nails to peel them off. This takes longer but does not expose the nuts to higher temperatures. Make sure to keep them wet after soaking and rinsing.

Glorious Garden Hi-Pro "Fundue" with Veggie "Chips"

Day 7

Yield: 2 servings

12 to 24 hours to soak
1 to 8 hours to dehydrate (optional)
15 minutes to prepare

Blended almond "yogurt" with a high-protein choice of vegetables for dipping and dunking.

3 cups almonds (to make 1 cup almond "cheese" or 1 cup almond "yogurt")
Optional seasonings:
Mustard or nutritional yeast and miso, to taste
Veggie "Chips":
Sliced broccoli flowers and stalks, celery, green and purple cabbage, jicama, yams, bell peppers, yellow squash, lettuce, or any fresh vegetable in season you enjoy

1. Soak the almonds for 12 to 24 hours; rinse.

2. To make almond "yogurt," blanch the soaked, rinsed almonds. (See the next-day preparation notes on page 41 for more detailed instructions.) In a blender, process the almonds in enough water to cover, adding more water to thin to a consistency like keifer. Pour the mixture into a strainer held over a glass bowl or a wide-mouthed jar. This fluid will become the most lovely "yogurt" by morning.

3. To make almond "cheese", take the almond meal that has been strained, put it into a sprouting bag or natural fiber cloth bag, and continue to squeeze out the remaining

moisture. Let set on a counter overnight in the bag, or place in a colander lined with cheese cloth that is set in a bowl to catch any additional "whey." Wrap the cloth around the almond meal, and place a weight on top to press it further.

4. In the morning, the "yogurt" and almond "cheese" will be ready. They can be eaten as is or spiced with mustard or nutritional yeast and miso and used as a sauce or dip.

5. Cut vegetables up into "chips," and serve with the "yogurt" dip or the more spreadable "cheese."

6. To serve warm, place the entire blended mixture in a glass pie plate and then into a dehydrator for 1 to 2 hours at 105°F, warming to the temperature you desire. (If you prefer, "yogurt" left in the dehydrator all night acquires a consistency like mousse and the "cheese" becomes more like ricotta.)

Ingredient Options: Almonds are very rich in calcium, which is more easily assimilated into our systems without heating or treating the almonds before eating them. Sunflower seeds can also be used to make a "yogurt" or "cheese" as well. They have different flavors and textures than those made with almonds, but the sunflower seeds do not need to be skinned.

For those who do well with fruit in the morning, fruit "chips" could be substituted, and the spicing of the "yogurt" or "cheese" could be sweetened with honey or maple syrup and cinnamon. Let your mind go wild, creating choices of fruits or vegetables.

Machine Options: A Vita-Mix is the machine I prefer for this recipe. It grinds the almonds into a finer consistency than a blender, however, a regular blender can be used. Be sure to blend long enough to get a smooth consistency. To do this, you can add the nuts first, with less water, and blend to a smooth consistency, then add the rest of the water.

I have used a grater for slicing the veggies or apples into "chips," and cookie cutters can also make fun shapes for fruits or vegetables. Have fun making the food look lovely or appealing to the eye as well as the tongue.

Warming Options: The dehydrator does the best job of warming the almond cheese or yogurt. It can be used after the fermenting or as part of the fermenting process.

Lunch Choices

Day 1—Creamy Squash Soup, Bush Broccoli Salad, & Blushing Vinaigrette Dressing

A creamy, spicy warmed soup and protein-rich, crunchy salad—a luncheon to delight your eyes as well as your palate.

Soup: cashews, squash, red onions, curry powder, olive oil, parsley, lemon;

Salad: butter leaf lettuce, broccoli, tomato, green onions;

Dressing: tomato, basil, parsley, celery, apple cider vinegar.

Day 2—Sunned Patty & Lightly Lemoned Coleslaw

A veggie burger seasoned softly, accompanied by a colorful coleslaw— phytochemically full.

Patty: carrots, beet, sunflower seeds, green onion, parsley, dulse;

Garnish: romaine lettuce, sprouts, red onion rings, tomato and cucumber slices;

Coleslaw: carrots, cabbage, lemon juice, dill weed, caraway seed, kelp.

Day 3—Celebration Loaf with Darrell's Cilantro Special Salad

A calcium-filled loaf to celebrate lunch or dinner, accompanied by a lettuce-less salad of crunchy and munchy vegetables and sprouts.

Loaf: carrots, almonds, sunflower seeds, garlic clove, celery, yellow onion, parsley, bell pepper, Spike;

Salad: cilantro, green cabbage, mung bean sprouts, tomatoes;

Dressing: cilantro, almonds, lemon juice, Bragg Liquid Aminos.

Day 4—Eggplant "Pizza" with Creamy Spinach Soup

This wheat-free "unfloured" pizza will delight your eyes as well as your mouth— washed down with surprisingly spiced creamy soup.

"Pizza": eggplant, fresh and dried tomatoes, olive oil, garlic, fresh basil, pitted dates, avocado, squash, carrot, parsley;

Soup: spinach, cucumbers, green onions, garlic, avocado, bell pepper, dulse, kelp, spearmint leaves.

Day 5—Cauliflower Casserole with Autumn Salad & Green Goddess Dressing

This could-be-couscous casserole of cauliflower is blessed with a brightly colored creamy dressed salad.

Casserole: cauliflower, canola oil, Spike, parsley, thyme, oregano, yellow onion;

Salad: red leaf lettuce, celery, bell pepper, carrots;

Dressing: avocado, green onion, lemon juice, bell pepper.

Day 6—Pecaned Pâté with Veggie "Chips"

As a dip or as a nutty way to eat lunch, your mouth will say yes to this pâté and "chips."

Pâté: pecans, red onions, poultry spice, Celtic salt, basil, parsley;

Veggie "chips": romaine lettuce leaves, cabbage, red pepper, cucumber.

Day 7—Broccoli Soup with Golden Spinach Salad & Lemon Dill Dressing

Broccoli has never tasted so fine and felt so good going into your tummy with such a lovely, light spinach salad—so refreshingly dressed.

Soup: broccoli, avocado, onion, bell pepper, parsley, Bragg Liquid Aminos;

Salad: spinach, sprouts, carrots, yellow squash;

Dressing: lemon, cucumber, dill weed, extra-virgin olive oil, mustard powder, celery.

ℋ word about lunch

There are days when eating a warmed food for lunch is just what the mouth and stomach ordered. Salads traditionally are not warmed, and yet there are instances when a salad dressing is warmed and poured over spinach or other greens. This certainly is an option here as well.

Soups lend themselves to several warming techniques: either warming the broth and pouring it over grated raw vegetables or warming up the entire batch. Both certainly are options. I have used an electric skillet or a stove top skillet to warm. The Vita-Mix, if used to blend, certainly does warm up any-thing it blends for a while—less than six minutes in my experience. You can also use a warming plate made for glass coffee pitchers. I have found that soups can be warmed on this as well, but watch them carefully; the plates will heat high enough to cook the soups.

A dehydrator can be used at 105°F or lower to maintain enzyme content. The pecanned pâté, which can be formed into patties and warmed, are delicious. There are other dishes that you can experiment with, as well, to see if you pre-fer them warmed in a dehydrator. It does take longer and needs to be monitored the first few times to see how long it will take to warm the food up. In some areas (the desert, for instance) less time is needed. Near the beach or in very wet, cold climates, a longer dehydration time will be required to bring the food up to a warmed temperature or to the desired crispness.

Leaving food in a window, on a counter, or a ledge will allow the normal air flow through the room to warm it up. Sometimes even turning the oven on low, warming it up, shutting off the heat, and them putting the food in to warm can do wonders. Again, pay attention to the results. If you want a cooked food, do it. If not, then watch to see how you can keep more of the enzymes intact and a part of your meal.

Feel free to use any of the recipes in the lunch or dinner sections for either of those two meals—eat dinner for lunch or the other way around. Or, if you prefer, eat just one or the other. There are many days when I eat only breakfast and then either a lunch or dinner, and it is plenty of food. A fruit snack or a vegetable munch might tide me through if I get hungrier.

Creamy Squash Soup

Day 1

Yield: 4 to 6 servings

20 minutes to prepare

This creamy soup is colorfully spiced to warm the eyes as well as the tummy.

1 to 2 teaspoons extra-virgin olive oil
1 to 2 teaspoons curry
1 clove garlic
¼ minced red onion
1 cup raw cashews
2 to 4 cups purified water
1½ to 2½ pounds yellow squash (enough for 2 to 4 cups, finely shredded)
4 tablespoons fresh parsley
Bragg Liquid Aminos or Celtic salt, to taste
1 lemon

1. In an electric skillet (such as a Rival brand), warm the olive oil, curry powder, and garlic, keeping the temperature on warm or low.

2. Add the minced red onion, and allow the flavors to blend for 2 to 4 minutes.

3. In a blender, puree the cashews and water until creamy. This will make your soup stock. (Add less water for a richer stock, more for a thinner stock.)

4. In a food processor fitted with an "S" blade, chip the yellow squash into small pieces until fully shredded.

5. Add the squash and the soup stock to the electric skillet, and gradually warm to serving temperature, adding the parsley, Bragg or Celtic salt, and lemon juice.

Ingredient Options: I have made a number of variations on this rich and warm soup. You can cut back on the cashews and add red miso (a soybean paste) to the broth and make this a much saltier soup. If you prefer, you can make the broth with pine nuts and spice it with cumin powder. Green zucchini can be used instead of the yellow squash. I love serving this with a slice of lemon on top, garnished with parsley.

Machine Options: A large porcelain, glass, or stainless steel skillet could be used on the stove, but you need to keep the temperature very low. Don't cook—warm. As long as you can keep your finger in the soup, it's not too hot.

Warming Options: An electric skillet does the best job. Set it as low as it will go and still be turned on. You can also use a saucepan on a stove top. Take it off if it gets too hot.

Notes

Bush Broccoli Salad

Day 1

Yield: 2 servings

15 minutes to prepare

This protein-rich salad will add crunch to your lunch.

1 stalk broccoli
2 green onions, thinly sliced
½ to 1 head butter leaf lettuce, washed and torn
2 tomatoes, thinly sliced

1. Peel off the outer layer of the broccoli stalks, and slice thinly like cucumbers. Save the flowerettes for garnishing.

2. Add the onions and torn lettuce leaves.

3. Toss and dress with lemon or lime juice, or use the Blushing Vinaigrette dressing on the next page. Garnish with the broccoli flowerettes centered on top of the tomato slices.

Blushing Vinaigrette Dressing

Day 1

Yield: 1½ to 2 cups

15 minutes to prepare

A warmly spiced, "blushing" vinaigrette.

½ to 1 cup apple cider vinegar
2 to 3 fresh tomatoes
4 to 6 dried tomatoes soaked in warm water for 20 minutes
1 clove garlic
3 tablespoons fresh parsley
2 to 3 tablespoons fresh basil
2 stalks celery
Dulse and/or Celtic salt, to taste

1. In a blender, process the dressing ingredients, adding additional vinegar, garlic, parsley, basil, and dulse and/or Celtic salt to taste.

2. Toss with salad and enjoy.

Ingredient options: Popcorn Pizzazz and Tomato Tornado make this delightful—see page 136 in the resource section. If you like spice, add cayenne or a spicy little red or green chile pepper to warm up this dressing in a jiffy.

Sunned Patty

Day 2

Yield: 6 to 8 patties

12 hours to soak
15 minutes to prepare
6 to 12 hours to dehydrate (optional)

A veggie "burger" seasoned to perfection for your palate.

2 cups sunflower seeds
1 beet
3 carrots
1 cup finely minced parsley
1 green onion, finely minced
2 tablespoons Salt-Free Dash or red miso, to taste
Garnishes:
Romaine lettuce leaves, sprouts, red onion rings, tomato,
cucumber slices

1. Soak the sunflower seeds for 12 hours; rinse.

2. In a food processor fitted with an "S" blade, process the beet with the carrots and soaked sunflower seeds.

3. In a large bowl, combine the carrot mixture with the minced parsley, onion, and Dash to taste.

4. Form the mixture into patties 3 inches in diameter and ½ to 1 inch thick. Dehydrate at 105°F for 6 to 12 hours, turning over halfway through, or serve fresh on top of lettuce with the garnishes of your choice.

Ingredient Options: You can leave out the beet for a less pink patty or add red miso for a saltier patty. These can also be made without any parsley or onions. You could add mustard, mayonnaise, and other condiments on top. You can make these on a weekend and enjoy them throughout the week. They keep very well in the refrigerator. You can also make them into balls, croquettes, or loaves for simple variations.

Machine Options: The Champion or Green Power machines could be used as well, with the solid "blank" in place. These machines create a smoother texture.

Warming Options: These patties can be dehydrated on the porch or in a window or served fresh. They keep longer when they are dehydrated and taste best fresh out of the dehydrator.

Notes

Lightly Lemoned Coleslaw

Day 2

Yield: 6 to 8 servings

20 minutes to prepare

Filled with phytochemicals, this coleslaw will help you ward off cancer.

¼ head green cabbage
¼ head purple cabbage
2 carrots
1 cup fresh dill weed

Dressing:
Kelp, to taste
1 teaspoon dill seed
1 teaspoon caraway seed
½ cup lemon juice

1 lemon, sliced, for garnish

1. In a food processor with a grating attachment, grate the cabbage and carrots, and toss in a large bowl. (You can also grate the vegetables on a hand grater or chop finely by hand.)

2. Finely chop the dill weed (save some for garnishing), and toss with the grated vegetables.

3. To make the dressing, add the kelp, dill seed, and caraway seed to the lemon juice, adjusting the amounts to suit your taste. I grind the dill and caraway seeds right before using—the bouquet is divine—but you can buy them pre-ground.

4. Toss the dressing into the salad, and chill. Serve garnished with some of the reserved fresh chopped dill weed and lemon slices.

Ingredient Options: You can make the dressing just with lemon juice and Tomato Tornado (see page 133) or Celtic salt. One color of cabbage is fine—I enjoy both for the flavor as well as their color. Cabbage is rich in phytochemicals that help to protect our body from cancer. If dill weed isn't in season, parsley can be used instead.

Machine Options: I'll use a hand grater if I want to make less or if I'm traveling. An electric citrus juicer makes lemon juicing much easier. However, you can also try this trick. Cut the lemon in half, and insert a fork into the pulp, next to the skin. Twist it around the rim of the rind as you squeeze the lemon.

Warming Options: This dish can also be served warm by using your electric skillet or stove top pan, adding the dill and lemon juice after warming. Watch carefully so you don't overwarm.

Notes

Celebration Loaf

Day 3

Yield: 4 to 8 servings

8 to 10 hours to soak
10 minutes to prepare

A calcium-filled loaf to celebrate lunch or dinner with a friend.

1 cup sunflower seeds
1 cup almonds
1 clove garlic
2 carrots
2 stalks celery
½ yellow or red onion
1 red bell pepper
1 yellow bell pepper
1 cup parsley
Spike, to taste

1. Soak the sunflower seeds and almonds for 8 to 10 hours; rinse.

2. In a food processor fitted with an "S" blade, process the sunflower seeds, almonds, garlic, and carrots.

3. Finely dice the celery, onion, bell peppers, and parsley.

4. Mix all the ingredients together, adding Spike to taste. Form into a loaf and garnish with additional parsley, if you like.

Ingredient Options: You can add a beet for a pinker loaf. If you want to make this even tastier, baste the top with a raw tomato sauce (fresh and/or dried tomatoes blended with garlic and olive oil). For a sweeter version, blend in 2 pitted dates and 6 fresh basil leaves. I also enjoy making this recipe into balls, croquettes, or patties and serving them garnished with fresh tomato and cucumber slices.

Machine Options: The Champion or Green Power machines can be used, as well, with the solid "blank" in place. These machines create a smoother texture.

Warming Options: This loaf can be dehydrated on the porch, in a window, or put into the dehydrator at 105°F to warm for 4 to 8 hours. It is tasty enough to be served as is.

Notes

Darrell's Cilantro Special Salad

Day 3

Yield: 2 servings

20 minutes to prepare

For those folks who want a salad without the lettuce.

1 bunch cilantro
2 cups sliced green cabbage
1 carrot, grated
1 cup mung bean sprouts
2 tomatoes, sliced

1. Either pull off the cilantro leaves or chop the stalks and leaves (saving some cilantro leaves for garnish); place in a bowl.

2. Add the sliced cabbage, grated carrot, and sprouts, and toss together.

3. Toss and dress the salad with lemon or lime juice, or use the Creamy Cilantro Dressing on the next page. Garnish with cilantro leaves centered on top of thin tomato slices.

Creamy Cilantro Dressing

Day 3

Yield: 1½ to 2 cups

8 to 12 hours to soak
15 minutes to prepare

The almonds add lycine and calcium to this creamy dressing.

1 bunch cilantro
½ cup almonds
½ to ¾ cup fresh lemon juice
Bragg Liquid Aminos or Celtic salt, to taste
½ to 1 cup purified water

1. Soak the almonds for 8 to 12 hours; rinse.

2. In a blender, process all the ingredients, adjusting the amount of lemon juice and Bragg to taste and thinning to the desired consistency with water.

3. Toss with salad and enjoy.

Eggplant "Pizza"

Day 4

Yield: 2 to 4 servings

1 to 2 hours to dehydrate/sun
20 minutes to soak
20 minutes to prepare

A flourless pizza to thrill wheat-sensitive eaters.

1 eggplant

Sauce:
½ cup dried tomatoes
2 to 3 tablespoons olive oil
1 clove garlic
¼ cup fresh basil
2 to 4 pitted dates

Toppings:
1 sliced avocado
1 cup grated yellow squash
½ cup grated carrot
4 tablespoons chopped fresh parsley

1. Peel and slice the eggplant into ½-inch thick rounds. Place in a dehydrator at 105°F.

2. To make the sauce, soak the dried tomatoes in enough warm water to cover for 20 minutes, then pour the soaking water into a blender with the soaked tomatoes. Add the olive oil and crushed garlic, and puree. Add the basil and pitted dates, and puree again until creamy.

3. Put the sauce on top of the sliced eggplant, and let dehydrate (or sun-dry) for 1 to 2 hours.

4. Just before serving, decorate with toppings on each slice, return to the dehydrator for 5 to 10 minutes, and serve warm.

Ingredient Options: Toppings can be changed to suit your taste. You can use black olives, onion slices, basil, and mushrooms, just as you would any pizza.

Machine Options: A regular blender does just fine for the sauce, although a Vita-Mix can also be used.

Warming Options: The sun will dehydrate the eggplant, but a dehydrator will work regardless of the weather. It tastes best fresh out of the dehydrator.

Notes

Creamy Spinach Soup

Day 4

Yield: 4 to 6 servings

15 minutes to prepare

Even Popeye would sing for this enzyme-packed soup.

1 avocado
1 cup water
2 unwaxed cucumbers
1 cup spinach
2 green onions
1 clove garlic
⅓ yellow bell pepper
Dulse and kelp, to taste
4 to 6 fresh spearmint leaves

1. In a blender, add the avocado and ½ the water first, puree, then add the crunchier items (except the mint leaves), one at a time, blending to the desired thickness and thinning with the remaining water, if desired. Flavor with dulse and kelp to taste.

2. Serve in soup bowls, garnished with fresh mint leaves.

Ingredient Options: I first made this soup in a dinner workshop entitled "Eating in the Raw Around the World." It is fashioned after a Hungarian soup recipe. You can make this a richer soup, if you like, by adding tahini (sesame seeds blended into a "butter"-like consistency). Red bell pepper can be substituted for the yellow bell pepper. You can replace the garlic with lemon juice. Red or yellow onions can be used instead of green onions. Romaine can be added for extra greens (more chlorophyll).

Machine Options: I actually prefer using a Vita-Mix for this recipe instead of a blender, because it is easier to just throw everything in together with little cutting, use the tamper stick, and blend.

Warming Options: In the Vita-Mix, the longer you blend, the warmer the soup gets. If you don't have a Vita-Mix, this soup can be warmed carefully either in an electric or stove top skillet on low heat.

Notes

Cauliflower Casserole

Day 5

Yield: 4 to 6 servings

20 minutes to prepare

This could-be-couscous casserole warms your eyes as well as your tummy.

**1 to 2 teaspoons canola oil
2 to 4 teaspoons cumin
1 to 2 teaspoons turmeric
½ yellow onion, finely minced
1 cup purified water
Flowerets from 1 very large or 2 smaller cauliflowers
4 tablespoons minced fresh parsley
½ cup minced red bell pepper
Granulated garlic, to taste
Salt-free Spike, to taste**

1. In an electric skillet, warm the canola oil, cumin, and turmeric.

2. Keeping the temperature on warm or low, add the onion and allow the flavors to blend for 2 to 4 minutes, then add the water and warm.

3. In a food processor fitted with an "S" blade, process the cauliflower into small pieces.

4. Add the cauliflower to the skillet, and gradually warm, adding the parsley, bell pepper, garlic, and Spike, garnishing with additional parsley, if you like.

Cauliflower Casserole

Ingredient Options: Ed Douglas originally made a version of this with butter, salt, and pepper, like mashed potatoes. I have made it into a casserole with a number of variations. Adding bell peppers can add color and more moisture. If you want a saltier version, add brown rice miso or barley miso (a soybean paste) to Step 2. You can make it more like a soup by blending the casserole once warmed and adding warm water to thin to the desired consistency. Other seasonings can be substituted for Spike, such as Italian, Mexican, or curry blends, or just black pepper.

Machine Options: A Rival skillet or a stove top saucepan will do.

Warming Options: A large skillet could be used on the stove, but you need to keep the temperature very low. Don't cook—warm. As long as you can keep your finger in the soup, it's not too hot.

Notes

From upper left: Rye Bread Sticks, pages 114-115, Brainy Breakfast Chowder, pages 32-33, and Eggplant "Pizza," pages 60-61

Autumn Salad

Day 5

Yield: 2 servings

15 minutes to prepare

Red, yellow, and orange dress your bowl with autumn in mind.

½ yellow bell pepper
½ red bell pepper
2 stalks celery
1 carrot, grated
1 head green leaf lettuce, washed and torn into pieces

1. Slice the bell pepper and celery into bite-size pieces, and put into a bowl.

2. Add the grated carrot and lettuce.

3. Toss and dress the salad with lemon or lime juice, or use the Green Goddess Dressing on the next page, garnishing with additional grated carrots and bell pepper slices.

Ingredient Options: A lovely touch for this salad is to cut the bell pepper into thin strips and dehydrate them to use for garnish.

Green Goddess Dressing

Day 5

Yield: 1 to 1½ cups

15 minutes to prepare

1 avocado
2 green onions
½ red bell pepper
¼ to ½ cup fresh lemon juice
Dulse or kelp, to taste
½ to 1 teaspoon cumin
½ to 1 cup purified water

1. In a blender, process all the ingredients, adjusting the amounts of lemon juice, dulse or kelp, and cumin to taste. Thin to the desired consistency with additional water.

2. Toss with salad and enjoy.

Pecaned Pâté with Veggie "Chips"

Day 6

Yield: 4 to 6 servings

20 minutes to prepare

This delicately seasoned nut pâté is fit for royalty. Create playful shapes for the veggie "chips," and let their color dazzle your eyes

2 cups pecans
¼ to ½ red onion
1 teaspoon poultry spice
4 to 6 fresh basil leaves
¼ to ½ cup grated carrots, beets, and/or squash (optional)
½ cup finely minced parsley

Garnishes:
Romaine lettuce leaves
Purple and/or green cabbage chips
Red bell pepper wedges
Cucumber slices

1. In a food processor fitted with an "S" blade, blend the pecans, onion, poultry spice, and basil leaves. Thin with enough water to make a consistency like pâté. You can also omit the water, add the optional grated veggies into the processor, and blend for a short time to create a moister pâté. Stir in the minced parsley and adjust the seasonings to taste.

2. Cut the Romaine, cabbage, red bell pepper, and cucumber into chip-size pieces.

3. Serve the pâté on a platter surrounded by the veggie "chips."

Ingredient Options: I tasted a version of this recipe prepared by Ed Douglas, made into patties and warmed. Form into patties and dehydrate at 105°F for 4 to 8 hours, or to the desired warmth and "crispness." Mustard, mayonnaise, and other condiments can be added on top. Include the condiments you enjoy. This recipe can also be made into a stuffing for red, orange, or yellow bell peppers. Green bell peppers aren't ripe and are difficult for many people to digest. Stuffing this pâté into celery boats or tomatoes is another tasty way to eat it. You can make this on a weekend and eat it as a pâté or patties throughout the week. It keeps very well in the refrigerator. You can also make it into balls, croquettes, or loaves for other variations.

Machine Options: The Champion or Green Power machines could be used, as well, with the solid "blank" in place. These machines create a smoother texture than a food processor.

Warming Options: The patties can be dehydrated on a porch or in a window or served fresh. They keep longer if they are dehydrated at 105°F for 4 to 8 hours. The pâté could also be warmed lightly in an electric or stove top skillet for a short while.

Notes

Broccoli Soup

Day 7

Yield: 4 servings

15 minutes to prepare

Broccoli has never tasted so creamy and smooth as in this lovely soup.

2 to 4 cups water
3 to 4 cups chopped broccoli
1 red bell pepper, cut in large pieces
½ red or yellow onion, cut in large pieces
1 avocado
¼ cup minced parsley
1 to 2 stalks celery, cut in large pieces
Kelp, dulse, or Celtic salt, to taste

1. In an electric skillet, warm 2 cups of the water, keeping the temperature at or below 118°F. Add the chopped broccoli, and warm for 5 minutes.

2. In a blender, puree the warmed broccoli, bell pepper, onion, avocado, parsley, and celery, thinning with additional water if necessary to achieve the desired consistency.

3. Serve warm, flavoring with kelp or dulse to taste.

Ingredient Options: I have made a number of variations on this rich and warm soup. You can cut back on the avocado and add yellow or white miso (a soybean paste) to make this a much saltier soup. If you prefer, you can make the soup richer by adding tahini (sesame seed butter). For a treat, blend a dehydrated bell pepper into the soup. You can spice this differently by adding cumin or ginger. I love serving this with a slice of lemon on top.

Machine Options: You can use an electric skillet to warm and a regular blender or a Vita-Mix to smooth and blend together.

Warming Options: A large skillet could be used on the stove, but you need to keep the temperature very low. Don't cook; you only need to warm the food. As long as you can keep your finger in the soup, it's not too hot. That is always your most accurate thermometer. If it's too hot for your finger, you're cooking the food. If you process it in a Vita-Mix long enough, it will warm that way as well.

Golden Spinach Salad

Day 7

Yield: 2 servings

15 minutes to prepare

Enjoy the fresh, green taste of all the ingredients and dressing designed to tickle your taste buds.

1 yellow squash, grated
¼ cup pine nuts
2 cups chopped spinach
2 tomatoes, thinly sliced
1 cup alfalfa sprouts

1. Put the squash, pine nuts, and washed spinach into a bowl.

2. Toss and dress with lemon or lime juice, or use the Lemon Dill Dressing below. Garnish with the tomato slices and alfalfa sprouts.

Lemon Dill Dressing

Yield: 1½ to 2 cups

15 minutes to prepare

½ cup dill weed
1 unwaxed cucumber
¼ to ½ cup extra-virgin olive oil
2 stalks celery
½ to 1 cup lemon juice
½ to 1 teaspoon mustard powder (Stone ground mustard could be used instead of mustard powder.)

1. In a blender, process all the ingredients, adjusting the amount of lemon juice and mustard powder to taste and thinning with water, if desired.

2. Toss with salad and enjoy.

Dinner Choices

Day 1—Stuffed Peppers & Creamy Thousand Island Dressing with A Grate Salad & Better Beet Dressing

A grate way to enjoy salad with peppers stuffed with spiced carrot pulp and loaded with fresh veggies.

Stuffed pepper: orange and red bell pepper, celery, red onion, parsley, carrot pulp, sea salt;

Creamy Dressing: sunflower seeds, tomatoes, celery, basil, parsley, Bragg Liquid Aminos, lemon juice;

Salad: alfalfa sprouts, grated carrots, yams, beets;

Beet Dressing: beets, soaked sunflower seeds, lemon juice.

Day 2—"Squabetti" Squash with Simply Italian Salad & Basic Italian Dressing

A delightfully bright, light new way to eat squash with an Italian salad spiced to perfection.

Squabetti: squash, flax oil, Tomato Tornado, parsley, fresh tomatoes;

Salad: tomato, yellow or white onion rings, fresh basil;

Dressing: lemon juice, olive oil, garlic, kelp.

Day 3—Tostada with Salsa & Guacamole

Oh yeah, José, a wheat-free, dairy-free tostada with such a spicy salsa and "mucho bueno" guacamole.

Tortillas: barley, sea salt, cumin;

Tostada topping: jicama, celery, red and yellow bell pepper, green onions, green and purple cabbage, clover sprouts, romaine lettuce;

Salsa: tomatoes, garlic, lime, green onions, tomatillos, chili, cilantro;

Guacamole: avocado, tomato, cumin, lemon, Mexican seasoning.

Day 4—Tabouli with Royal Tahini Dip

Tabouli with a twist of lemon and a luxurious purple tahini dip to accompany your Middle Eastern feast.

Tabouli: buckwheat, parsley, red onions, tomatoes, spearmint, lemon, olive oil, sea salt, romaine and green leaf lettuce;

Dip: Raw tahini, lemon, beet, Bragg Liquid Aminos;

Garnishes: Romaine lettuce, yellow bell pepper, cucumber.

Day 5—"Asparagusto" Soup with Orange U Glad It's Salad? & Tangy Orange Dressing

Enjoy this zinc-enriched soup and calcium-filled salad to improve your immune system.

Soup: red and yellow tomatoes, asparagus, basil, parsley, dried tomatoes, limes;

Salad: butter leaf lettuce, orange slices, celery, clover sprouts;

Dressing: orange juice, sunflower seeds, celery, parsley, dates, lime.

Day 6—Barley Warmed Casserole with Radishly Green Salad & Creamy Italian Dressing

A barley warmed casserole rich in vitamins and minerals with a creamy dressed salad to calm those frazzled nerves and soothe the tummy.

Casserole: barley, oat groats, tomatoes, red onion, lemon, cumin, parsley, zucchini, Bragg Liquid Aminos;

Salad: green leaf lettuce, radishes, alfalfa sprouts, avocado;

Dressing: Lemon, avocado, celery, basil, parsley, thyme, garlic, Popcorn Pizzazz.

Day 7—Unbaked Beans with Greens

A sprouted soybean salad rich in plant-based estrogens to feed your hormones as well as your mouth, plus a delightfully sprouted salad.

Beans: soybeans, kalamata olives, onion, garlic, sun-dried tomatoes, capers, lime, olive oil, chili, cayenne;

Greens: Sprouts, buckwheat greens, red leaf lettuce, carrots, lemon.

$\mathcal{A}$ word about dinner

A warmed food for dinner is divine, especially when it is cold outside. A warmed soup or main dish, a warmed bun or bread sticks can enhance the fragrance of any meal. As I've said earlier, lunch or dinner menus can be interchanged. If you want to eat dinner for lunch, fine. If one main meal a day is plenty for you, perfect.

Choosing organic produce is important. We are not only supporting an industry that ought to prosper, but we are helping to heal Mother Earth as well. It's a wonderful idea to either grow our own produce or shop at farmers' markets or other markets that stock organic produce. Make sure you wash all produce carefully. Parasites and other critters can stick to food and make an unwelcome addition to your meal. There are citrus sprays sold in most health food stores, or you can mix up a batch of your own with sea salt and lemon juice. The sodium chloride in the salt and the citric acid in the lemon juice combine to make a cleanser that works fine.

Another thought to share with you: The digestion of food is based on several factors. The first is the amount of time we spend chewing our food, because saliva starts the digestive process. Then the stomach needs to produce sufficient hydrochloric acid and other digestive juices to process our foods. It has also been suggested that there are other factors that enhance digestion, such as texturizing the food to make it simpler to break down. Some people feel that drinking juice at the start of a meal stimulates digestion. Others feel that high-quality salt (Celtic salt is one very fine example) enhances the cells' ability to move nutrients through the cell membrane. Without a proper chemical balance, our bodies have a tough time making ends meet. So instead of taking out the salt, consider adding Celtic salt to foods once they are prepared, and see if your system does better with the added trace minerals.

Another habit to get into is eating dinner earlier rather than later. I know this can be a challenge. It has been for me, as I often teach and get off work after 10 P.M. Other years I was living with a person who got off work at 8 P.M. We often didn't eat until after 9 P.M. If you are able to eat at or before 6 P.M., your body can rest better when you do go to sleep. Taking a walk, after or even before you do the dishes, can also stimulate digestion and enhance the process of assimilating your foods.

Let your body help you decide what foods are best for you. If you only want a salad or a soup for dinner, fine. If you are hungry, eat more. Lunch can be the biggest meal for some people; for others dinner is. See what works best for you. We all have lessons to learn around food and what is optimum for each of us. It is not about a rule or a system; it is about your body and what it needs.

In any event, make the last meal of your day a prayer, a gift to you from Mother Nature and those who helped to grow the food, who helped to get it to market, and who then prepared it lovingly. If you are upset, go rest and let yourself cool down first. I enjoy singing to my foods as I prepare them. Saying a prayer before each meal is certainly a loving way to start any meal. Whether it is a specific prayer or one you make up each time you sit down to eat, it sends off a vibration of gratitude that is heard and felt inside the body and adds a special ingredient to the meal—love.

Stuffed Peppers and Creamy Thousand Island Dressing

Day 1

Yield: 4 servings

8 to 12 hours to soak
25 minutes to prepare

The perfect solution for what to do with all that carrot pulp. It's a meal—what a deal.

1 orange bell pepper
2 stalks celery
½ red onion
½ cup parsley
1 to 2 teaspoons Celtic salt
2 cups carrot pulp
2 red bell peppers

Creamy Thousand Island Dressing:
¾ cup sunflower seeds
6 to 8 basil leaves
2 fresh tomatoes
6 tablespoons minced fresh parsley
2 stalks celery
Bragg Liquid Aminos, to taste
¼ to ½ cup fresh lemon juice
½ to 1 cup water

1. Soak the sunflower seeds for the Creamy Thousand Island Dressing overnight; drain.

2. Finely dice the orange bell pepper, celery, red onion and parsley for the salad, and place in a large bowl.

3. In a blender, process all the ingredients for the dressing using enough water to make a smooth consistency. Set aside some of the dressing ingredients before blending and several tablespoons of the dressing itself after blending to use as garnish.

3. Add the Celtic salt, carrot pulp, and dressing to the finely diced veggies, and toss.

4. Cut the red bell peppers in half, and stuff with the carrot and veggie mixture, garnishing with the reserved dressing ingredients and a dollop of dressing.

Ingredient Options: You can use a commercial soy-based mayonnaise if you don't want to make the dressing. Also, I love to add 2 tablespoons Tomato Tornado (see page 133) to the dressing. Serving this meal with carrot juice gives you the pulp.

Machine Options: A Vita-Mix works fine for the dressing.

Warming Options: The peppers can be warmed in an oven which has been turned to low, warmed, and turned off. Put the unstuffed bell peppers into the oven to warm, then remove and stuff. The filling can be warmed in either an electric or stove top skillet. Stuff into the peppers and serve.

A Grate Salad

Day 1

Yield: 2 servings

20 minutes to prepare

A grate way to dress up a salad—it almost "dresses" itself.

1 carrot, grated
1 beet, grated
½ yam, grated
1 cup alfalfa sprouts

1. Toss the grated carrot, beet, and yam in a bowl.

2. Dress with lemon or lime juice or use the Better Beet Dressing on the next page, garnishing with the alfalfa sprouts.

Better Beet Dressing

Day 1

Yield: 1½ to 2 cups

8 to 12 hours to soak
15 minutes to prepare

This calcium-rich dressing blushes with delight, ready to address any salad.

1 cup sunflower seeds
1 beet
½ to ¾ cup fresh lemon juice
Bragg Liquid Aminos, to taste
¼ to ½ cup water

1. Soak the sunflower seeds for 8 to 12 hours; rinse.

2. In a blender, process all the dressing ingredients, adjusting the amounts of lemon juice and Bragg to taste. Thin with the water to a desired consistency.

3. Toss with salad and enjoy.

"Squabetti" Squash

Day 2

Yield: 2 to 4 servings

10 minutes to prepare

A wheat-free, egg-free, fresh and lovely change for spaghetti lovers.

2 medium zucchini
1 red and 1 yellow tomato (or 2 of one color)
¼ cup parsley

Sauce:
2 to 3 tablespoons flax seed oil
3 to 5 teaspoons Tomato Tornado (see page 133)
½ cup finely minced parsley
Sea salt, to taste

1. Grate the squash lengthwise into a bowl, making a julienne cut or angel hair-sized pieces.

2. To make the sauce, combine the flax seed oil, Tomato Tornado powder, parsley, and sea salt. Toss into the squash.

3. Serve on a platter garnished with fresh parsley and thin tomato slices, if you like.

Ingredient Options: Flax seed oil contains omega-3 fatty acids which help to lower cholesterol and protect us from cancer. Olive oil could be substituted for flax oil, and dried or fresh tomatoes blended with garlic could be substituted for the Tomato Tornado. Add any other vegetable that you like to this dish.

Machine Options: Kim Sproul and Jamey Dina prepared this recipe during a guest appearance on my show. They had found a European grater that really made this dish work. After two years of looking, I found a grater that would produce the "angel hair" consistency, The Multi-Slice Grater (see page 135).

Warming Options: The squash could be warmed carefully with an electric or stove top skillet before adding the sauce.

Simply Italian Salad

Day 2

Yield: 2 servings

20 minutes to prepare

An Italian salad at its most basic, full of color and flavor.

2 to 3 tomatoes (Roma, Celebrity, or beefsteak are tasty)
6 to 10 fresh basil leaves
4 yellow or white onion rings

1. Thinly slice the tomatoes into rounds, and place on a platter.
2. Chop the basil leaves and use to garnish the tomatoes along with the onion rings.
3. Dress simply with lemon or lime juice, or use the Basic Italian Dressing below.

Basic Italian Dressing

Yield: 1½ to 2 cups

15 minutes to prepare

Fresh can be the best—taste the difference for yourself.

½ to ¾ cup fresh lemon juice
2 to 4 tablespoons extra-virgin olive oil
1 clove garlic
Kelp or Celtic salt, to taste
¼ to ½ cup purified water

1. In a blender, process all the dressing ingredients, adjusting the amounts of lemon juice and kelp or Celtic salt to taste. Thin to the desired consistency with the water.
2. Pour over salad and enjoy.

Tostada

Day 3

Yield: 8 servings

Tortillas: 8 hours to soak
(or 12 hours to soak and 24 hours to sprout)
15 minutes to prepare
4 to 8 hours to dehydrate

Tostadas:
25 minutes to prepare

---

*A totally fresh and alive version of a tostada. Enjoy the colors, the
enzymes, and the life force it gives back to you.*

Tortillas:
1½ cups pearled barley, or 1 cup sprouting barley
1 teaspoon Celtic salt
1 teaspoon cumin

Topping:
1 red and 1 yellow bell pepper
2 celery stalks
2 green onions
½ cup grated jicama
½ head romaine lettuce, torn into pieces
1 cup grated green cabbage
1 cup grated purple cabbage

Salsa, page 84
Guacamole, page 85

1. To make the tortillas, soak the pearled barley for 8 hours; rinse. If using sprouting barley, soak for 12 hours, then rinse and sprout for 24 hours.

2. In a blender, grind the soaked or sprouted barley, adding enough water (no more than 1 cup) to make a dough. Add the salt and cumin, and blend until chunky.

3. Put wax paper or teflex sheets on a dehydrator tray, and scoop out ¼ cup of the barley mixture for each tostada, flattening to circles 2 inches wide. Dehydrate for 4 to 8 hours at 105°F, turning and removing the wax paper or teflex sheet when the first side is no longer moist and the tortilla holds together. Keep them somewhat soft and chewy.

4. To make the topping, finely dice the bell peppers, celery, onions, and grated jicama.

5. To make a tostada, layer the lettuce, cabbage, and diced and grated vegetables on top of a tortilla, garnishing with guacamole and salsa.

Ingredient Option: If you're feeling lazy, use a lettuce leaf instead of a tortilla.

Notes

Salsa

Day 3

Yield: 3 cups sauce

15 minutes to prepare

Mild or spicy, the choice is yours for this salsa.

5 tomatoes
1 clove garlic
2 green onions
3 tomatillos
1 teaspoon chili powder
Juice of 1 lime
Bragg Liquid Aminos, to taste
Jalapeño, to taste (optional)
¼ cup finely diced fresh cilantro

1. In a food processor, chop all the ingredients except the cilantro until chunky, adjusting the amounts of chili powder, lime juice, Bragg, and jalapeño to taste.

2. Stir in the cilantro and let set for 30 minutes to allow the flavors to blend.

Guacamole

Day 3

Yield: 2 to 3 cups

15 minutes to prepare

The cumin helps this guacamole become more digestible—what a deal.

Juice of 1 lemon
1 tomato
3 avocados
½ teaspoon Mexican seasoning
(chili powder, oregano, garlic, etc.)
Cumin, to taste

1. In a food processor fitted with an "S" blade, blend the lemon juice with ½ the tomato and ½ the avocado until chunky.

2. Finely dice the remaining ½ tomato. Mash the remaining avocado, leaving the pulp chunky.

3. Combine both mixtures, seasoning with Mexican seasoning, cumin, and additional lemon juice to taste, if desired.

Tabouli

Day 4

Yield: 4 to 6 servings

8 to 12 hours to soak

20 minutes to prepare

Alive with flavor and vitamins, this tabouli is a keeper in your kitchen.

1½ cups buckwheat or oat groats

2 cups parsley

½ red onion

2 tomatoes

½ cup spearmint leaves

½ head romaine lettuce, leaves torn

½ green leaf lettuce, torn

Dressing:

Juice of 1 lemon

3 to 4 tablespoons olive oil

Celtic salt, to taste

1. Soak the buckwheat or oat groats overnight; rinse.

2. Finely dice the parsley, red onion, tomatoes, and spearmint leaves, and toss together with the rinsed barley or oats in a large bowl.

3. To make the dressing, mix the lemon juice with the olive oil and salt in a separate bowl. Toss with the salad and let set for 20 minutes to blend the flavors. Add the torn lettuce leaves, and serve.

Ingredient Options: Buckwheat can be found raw; look for a pale colored "grain," not a dark or toasted color. Oat groats or sprouting barley can be substituted for the buckwheat. Traditionally this dish is made with cracked wheat. A sprouted wheat berry could also be used; it takes 24 hours to soak and sprout. There are many other vegetables you could add: squash, cabbage, or your choice.

Machine Options: A Vita-Mix or a food processor fitted with an "S" blade could be used to blend the grain, if you use a heavier grain like barley or wheat.

Warming Options: After soaking the buckwheat or oats, lightly dehydrate them. (The buckwheat will get quite crunchy very quickly, so watch it carefully the first time you do this.) In the desert, I found I could dehydrate the buckwheat in less than 2 hours; it could take longer if you live somewhere more humid.

Royal Tahini Dip

Day 4

Yield: 2 cups sauce

15 minutes to prepare

Purple—the color of royalty. Treat yourself to this calcium-rich dip.

1 cup raw tahini
1 beet
Juice of 2 lemons
Bragg Liquid Aminos, to taste

Optional veggies:
4 romaine lettuce leaves
1 yellow bell pepper, cut in wedges
1 sliced cucumber

1. In a blender, process the tahini and beet, thinning down with water, if needed, to make a dipping consistency. Add the lemon juice and the Bragg to taste.

2. Serve with tabouli, or use as a dip with lettuce leaves, bell pepper wedges, and sliced cucumber.

Ingredient Options: Parsley and celery can also be blended into this dip. The beet can be left out, making the color more beige. For a spicier sauce, add a clove of garlic.

Machine Options: A Vita-Mix could be used to blend the dip.

Warming Options: The longer this is blended in a Vita-Mix, the warmer it gets. (Caution: Tahini gets very bitter when warmed in the dehydrator.)

"Asparagusto" Soup

Day 5

Yield: 2 to 4 servings

10 minutes to prepare

Zinc-rich—fortify your immune system with this lovely soup.

10-12 medium stalks asparagus
6 to 8 large red tomatoes
4 to 8 fresh basil leaves
1 cup fresh parsley
4 dried tomatoes
2 limes, cut into slices
4 to 6 large yellow tomatoes

1. Trim the tips from the asparagus, and set aside for garnish. In a blender, process 5 of the red tomatoes with the remaining asparagus, the basil, parsley, and dried tomatoes. Place slices of lime on the bottom of the soup bowls, and pour the asparagus mixture over.

2. In a blender, puree the 3 yellow tomatoes, and pour the puree around the outer edge of the soup.

3. Garnish with more lime slices, the remaining red tomato cut into slices, the asparagus tips, and additional basil and parsley, if desired. Chill or serve at room temperature.

Ingredient Options: Fresh, vine-ripened tomatoes taste so much better than most of what we get in the market. Find a farmers' market, or better yet, grow your own. Different varieties of tomatoes have their own unique flavors. I have found Japanese, Celebrity, and roma tomatoes are the best. The yellow tomatoes are more for a color contrast, as well as being lower in acid content. The good news is raw tomatoes are not acid forming; cooked ones are. This is a great cooling soup for a warm day.

Machine Options: A Vita-Mix or a food processor fitted with an "S" blade could be used to blend this soup.

Warming Options: Blend for a longer time in a Vita-Mix to warm up this soup.

Orange U Glad It's Salad?

Day 5

Yield: 4 servings

15 minutes to prepare

First eat with your eyes, then taste heaven on earth.

1 head butter leaf lettuce
½ cup clover sprouts
2 oranges, sliced into thin sections
2 stalks celery, thinly sliced

1. Wash the lettuce, leaving 4 leaves whole; tear up the rest into bite-sized pieces.

2. Fill the lettuce leaves with the lettuce pieces and clover sprouts. Top with the celery and orange sections.

3. Dress with plain orange juice or the Tangy Orange Dressing below.

Tangy Orange Dressing

Yield: 3 cups

15 minutes to prepare

1 to 1½ cups sunflower seeds
2 cups freshly squeezed orange juice
1 stalk celery
2 to 4 pitted dates
½ cup fresh parsley
Juice of 1 lime

1. Soak the sunflower seeds for 8 to 12 hours; rinse.

2. In a blender, puree the sunflower seeds, orange juice, celery, dates, parsley, and lime juice.

3. Chill and serve, or serve at room temperature. This is great as a dip also, thickened with more sunflower seeds.

Barley Warmed Casserole

Day 6

Yield: 4 to 6 servings

4 to 8 hours to soak
25 minutes to prepare

These are warming grains. On a cool day, let all the B vitamins calm your nerves.

2 cups barley
¾ cup oat groats
6 tomatoes
½ red onion, minced
1 to 2 teaspoons cumin
2 to 4 cups coarsely shredded green zucchini
Juice of 1 lemon
Bragg Liquid Aminos, to taste
4 tablespoons minced fresh parsley

1. Soak the barley and oat groats together for 4 to 8 hours; rinse.

2. In a food processor fitted with an "S" blade, coarsely cut first the barley, then the oats. Then coarsely shred the squash, and place in a separate bowl.

3. In the same food processor or a blender, puree 4 of the tomatoes until smooth.

4. In an electric skillet, combine the blended tomatoes, minced onion, and cumin, keeping the temperature on warm or low.

5. Stir the chopped barley and oats into the broth, adding the shredded squash, lemon juice, and Bragg, and continue to warm.

6. Serve warm, garnished with the minced parsley.

Ingredient Options: Thai peanut sauce is a treat with this casserole.

Machine Options: A Vita-Mix or food processor can be used to process the ingredients.

Warming Options: An electric or stove top skillet are possible, but you need to keep the temperature very low—don't cook, warm. As long as you can keep your finger in the casserole, it's not too hot.

Notes

Radishly Green Salad

Day 6

Yield: 2 servings
15 minutes to prepare

Tangy radishes coupled with creamy avocado make this a uniquely combined salad.

1 head green leaf lettuce
2 to 4 radishes
1 cup alfalfa sprouts
1 avocado

1. Wash and tear the lettuce into bite-sized pieces.

2. Slice the radishes and cut the sprouts.

3. Cut the avocado in half, remove the pit, and place each half on a bed of lettuce.

4. Garnish with the sprouts and radishes, squeezing lemon or lime juice on top, or use the Creamy Italian Dressing on the next page.

Creamy Italian Dressing

Day 6

Yield: 1½ to 2 cups

5 minutes to prepare

Lower your cholesterol with basil and garlic, a fine choice for us all.

¾ cup lemon juice
½ cup water
2 stalks celery
1 avocado
3 to 5 basil leaves
¼ cup fresh parsley
½ teaspoon thyme
1 clove garlic
Bragg Liquid Aminos or Celtic salt, to taste
Freshly ground pepper, to taste

1. In blender, puree all the ingredients, adjusting the spice amounts to taste, if you like.

2. Pour over salad and enjoy.

Ingredient options: One tablespoon of Tomato Tornado makes this delightful (see page 133).

Unbaked Beans

Day 7

Yield: 4 to 6 servings

2½ days to soak and sprout
15 minutes to prepare

Soy estrogens at their best, sprouted and ready to warm up and eat.

1¼ cups soybeans

Sauce:
**½ cup minced kalamata olives (pitted, soaked overnight,
and rinsed)**
½ yellow onion
1 clove garlic
2 tablespoons capers, rinsed
½ cup soaked sun-dried tomatoes
Juice of 1 lime
¼ cup extra-virgin olive oil
Chili powder and cayenne, to taste

1. Soak the soybeans in enough water to cover for 8 to 12 hours, then sprout for two days, rinsing often to keep the sprouts fresh.

2. To make the sauce, process the minced olives, onion, garlic, and capers in a food processor with the soaked dried tomatoes, lime juice, and olive oil and the chili and cayenne to taste.

3. Mix the sprouted beans and sauce in a bowl. If desired, carefully warm the sauce in an electric skillet, stir in the sprouted beans, and serve warm.

Ingredient Options: This dish was first prepared on one of my TV shows with a talented raw food chef, Rhio. I must admit, beans are not my favorite food, but this dish was quite tasty, and because the soy is sprouted, I did not have problems with gas at all from this dish. Black soybeans are a special treat if used in this dish. See page 136 for information on where to get them. Black olives could be substituted for the kalamata olives.

Machine Options: A Vita-Mix could be used to blend the sauce, if you want it very smooth.

Warming Options: Warmed lightly in an electric or stove top skillet, this is a wonderful tummy warmer.

Greens

Day 7

Yield: 4 servings

20 minutes to prepare

Green gives us chlorophyll and life—live it up with greens.

½ cup alfalfa sprouts
½ cup clover sprouts
½ cup buckwheat greens
4 red and/or green lettuce leaves
½ cup chopped bok choy
1 carrot, grated
Juice of 1 lemon or lime

1. Cut up the sprouts and serve on the lettuce leaves surrounded by the chopped bok choy and grated carrot.

2. Dress with lemon or lime juice.

Dessert Choices

Day 1—Almond Cookies

> *A simply divine chewy dessert of almonds, dried pineapple, papaya, and lemon.*

Day 2—Rainbow Sorbet

> *A frozen fruit treat of fresh bananas and blueberries, frozen blueberries, strawberries, bananas, and pineapple, and fresh mint leaves.*

Day 3—Pecan Mousse

> *Pecans and dates blended and dehydrated into the fluffiest mousse, complemented with a cranberried applesauce and covered with a gently warmed current sauce with cinnamon and gingerroot.*

Day 4—Strawberry Cream Pie

> *Ripe red strawberries sweetened to perfection smothered in banana-date-lemon-kiwi sauce in a pie crust of "toasty" almonds, dates, and raisins.*

Day 5—Date Nut Torte

> *A torte of walnuts, filberts, raisins, and currants, divinely topped with a lemon-date frosting—to live for.*

Day 6—"Unbaked" Apple

> *A gently warmed, delectably spiced apple delight to warm your tummy on cool wintry nights, with dried figs, apricots, cinnamon sticks, cloves, nutmeg, and lemon.*

Day 7—Hawaiian Treats

> *Macadamia nuts sweetened and rolled into balls of delight with apple and raisins.*

Top: Pecan Mousse, pages 102-103; Bottom: Strawberry Cream Pie, pages 104-105

A word about dessert

Typically, desserts are rich in fat, loaded with sugar, and eaten at the end of a meal. I am going to make a revolutionary suggestion. How about eating your dessert at the beginning of your meal? How about a dessert that not only has a low fat content but contains the enzymes to digest that fat? Finally, what about a dessert that has sugars that are natural to the body and do not stop your immune system from functioning (which white sugar does)? What a deal!

So, whether you choose fruit or fruit and nuts combined to enjoy before your meal, your digestive system will thank you for making the decision to eat dessert either first or on its own, at a separate time of day apart from your meals.

Obviously, any fresh fruit is a treat any time of the day. In the summer months there are more choices. Don't rule out dried fruits in the winter to supplement your diet and add natural sugar to your body. If you reconstitute dried fruits by soaking, you can add a lovely touch to the beginning of any meal. After all, fruits do digest quickly, and after twenty minutes or so, you can enjoy the advantage of having more food value from dried fruit than those fruits placed in storage and shipped a long distance. Organic is always the best, and homegrown produce has the advantage of being fresh picked. I had the privilege of living in a pecan orchard in New Mexico for a short time, and the white peaches and apples picked fresh from the trees remain dear in my memory.

There can be many variations on the same dessert. Sorbet, for example, can be made from almost any frozen fruit. Bananas make sorbet creamy, but mango and pineapple sorbets are certainly delicious on their own, without the bananas. Fruit pies can be filled with any fresh fruit in season, not just strawberries. Crusts can be made with any nut and dates or other dried fruits that you enjoy. Learning to play with the variations can be as exciting as making a dish from a recipe. Employ simple tricks, like thickening the filling with bananas, or using apples or blueberries (loaded with pectin that sets up and jells beautifully). Psyllium, flax seeds, or agar-agar (a seaweed thickener) can also be used to set up a filling. The simplest solution is to put the pie either in the refrigerator or freezer in warm months and the dehydrator during cool ones.

You are in for an adventure. Play with each recipe using different ingredients—a kind of theme and variation—and find your favorites. Include friends and family in the preparation, or surprise them and don't make a big deal over whether the dessert is cooked or not. They will taste and feel the difference. So will you. Bon appetite!

Unbaked Beans, pages 94-95

Almond Cookies

Day 1

Yield: 30 to 40 cookies

8 to 12 hours to soak
30 minutes to prepare
5 to 10 hours to dehydrate

*Enzyme-rich with bromelain and papain, these cookies will help digest
all your food.*

2 cups almonds
½ cup unsulfured, unsweetened dried pineapple
½ cup unsulfured, unsweetened dried papaya
Juice and zest of 1 lemon

1. Soak the almonds for 8 to 12 hours; rinse.

2. In a Vita-Mix or food processor fitted with an "S" blade, process the soaked almonds, dried pineapple and papaya, the lemon zest and juice, and enough water (not more than ½ cup) to moisten the resulting "dough."

3. Put the "dough" between two layers of wax paper, and roll out ½-inch thick. Make cookies using cookie cutters.

4. Place the cookies very close together on a dehydrator tray, and dehydrate at 105°F for 5 to 10 hours, or until they reach the desired crispness. For decoration, put an almond on top of each cookie.

Ingredient Options: This dough could be made with pecans, walnuts, or macadamias. Raisins, figs, dates, or apricots could also be used. Ginger, cinnamon, cardamom, or nutmeg can be used to spice the cookies. The pineapple and papaya have wonderful digestive enzymes, bromelain and papain, respectively. These enzymes help to digest proteins and fats and also help to reduce swelling in the body.

Machine Options: This cookie dough is so tasty you could eat it fresh and not dehydrate it. The Champion and Green Power machines can make this dough as well, using the solid "blank." A regular blender doesn't have the power to process the almonds adequately, however a food processor does the job fine.

Warming Options: Besides dehydrating, the cookies could also be put in the sunshine and sun-"baked," turning them over once.

Notes

Rainbow Sorbet

Day 2

Yield: 4 to 6 servings

8 to 12 hours to freeze fruit
20 minutes to prepare

Summer has such a fine array of fresh fruits. Freeze and enjoy this dairyless dessert.

9 bananas
1 pint blueberries
1 pint (1½ to 2 cups) strawberries, with hulls removed
1 pineapple, peeled and sliced
4 to 6 fresh mint leaves, plus more for garnish

1. Freeze 6 of the bananas, the blueberries, strawberries, and pineapple for at least 8 to 12 hours.

2. In a food processor fitted with an "S" blade, blend 2 of the frozen bananas, the blueberries, mint leaves, and 1 of the fresh bananas. Divide among 4 to 6 parfait glasses, and place the glasses in the freezer.

3. To make the second layer, blend 2 more of the frozen bananas with the frozen strawberries and 1 of the fresh bananas in the food processor. Spoon on top of the first layer, and return the glasses to the freezer.

4. To make the third layer, blend the 2 remaining frozen bananas, the frozen pineapple, and the remaining fresh banana in the food processor. Spoon on top of the second layer, garnish with additional fresh mint leaves, and serve immediately.

Ingredient Options: Each layer of this frozen dessert can be made and eaten separately. Any fresh fruit can be used; just blend with bananas—they make a smooth base.

Machine Options: Sorbet can be prepared with several machines. A Vita-Mix does just fine. The Champion and Green Power machines can do this as well, using the solid "blank."

Notes

Pecan Mousse

Day 3

Yield: 6 to 8 servings

20 minutes to prepare
8 to 10 hours to dehydrate

This tri-layered warm, fluffy mousse is a favorite at any time of the day or evening.

Bottom layer:
2 cups pecans
3 to 5 pitted dates
2 cups purified water

Sauce (middle layer):
1 apple
½ cup dried unsweetened cranberries
1 banana

Sauce (top layer):
2 cups currants
Fresh gingerroot, to taste
Cinnamon, to taste
½ to 1 cup purified water

1. In a blender, process the pecans and dates with the 2 cups water, adding additional water if needed to keep the mixture moving in the blender. Pour into a 9-inch glass pie plate.

2. To make the middle layer of sauce, puree the apple, cranberries, and banana in the blender. Pour into another 9-inch glass pie plate.

3. To make the top layer of sauce, puree the currants in the blender with the ginger-root, cinnamon, and enough of the water to make a pourable mixture. Pour into a third 9-inch glass pie plate.

4. Put the pie plates in a dehydrator set at 105°F for 8 to 10 hours, or until the mixture reaches a mousse-like consistency.

5. When the mousse and sauce layers are done, spoon one layer at a time into individual custard cups or parfait glasses. This is delicious served warm out of the dehydrator, or it can be chilled and served cool for summer occasions.

Ingredient Options: You can reverse the pecan-date layer with the apple-cranberry sauce, but keep the currant sauce on top.

Notes

Strawberry Cream Pie

Day 4

Yield: one 9-inch pie

12 to 24 hours to soak
25 minutes to prepare
1 to 2 hours to refrigerate or
2 to 4 hours to dehydrate crust
1 to 3 hours to refrigerate pie

The natural salicylate in strawberries is nature's pain killer. So work out to your heart's content, then serve up a slice of this pie for relief.

Crust:
2 cups almonds
4 to 6 pitted dates
½ cup raisins (optional)

Filling and Sauce:
6 bananas
1 teaspoon grated lemon zest
1 pint strawberries
½ cup date nuggets or pitted dates
1 kiwi, sliced

1. Soak the almonds for 12 to 24 hours; rinse.

2. To make the crust, grind the almonds, dates, and raisins (if using) to the consistency of moist meal in a food processor fitted with an "S" blade. Press into a 9-inch glass pie plate, and either place in a dehydrator for 2 to 4 hours at 105°F or refrigerate for 1 to 2 hours.

3. To make a sauce for the filling, process 2 of the bananas, the lemon zest, 4 of the strawberries, and the date nuggets in a blender. Set aside.

4. Line the crust with thin banana slices from 2 more of the bananas.

5. Set about ⅓ of a banana and a few strawberries aside for garnish. Mash the remaining bananas with a fork, and dice the remaining strawberries. Combine the mashed bananas and diced strawberries in a bowl with ½ of the filing sauce, and spoon on top of the pie crust.

6. Pour the remaining filling sauce on top of the mashed fruit, and garnish with rings of sliced kiwi, strawberries, and banana. Chill for 1 to 3 hours before serving.

Ingredient Options: The crust could be made with pecans or walnuts. Raisins, figs, or apricots could be substituted for the dates. Using edible flowers to decorate pies is a lovely touch. Your friends will truly be impressed with your skills.

Machine Options: You could simplify this recipe by not dehydrating the crust, or you could put the crust in the sun and warm it for a while, then chill it with the filling. The Champion and Green Power machines will both process the crust ingredients with the solid "blank" in place.

Notes

Date Nut Torte

Day 5

Yield: 12 to 14 servings

15 minutes to prepare
2 to 4 hours to dehydrate (optional)

This rich, sweet, luscious dessert is a four-star winner that is easy to prepare. Hardly a bite is left after any party.

Torte layers:
2 cups filberts (hazelnuts)
2 cups raisins
2 cups walnuts
2 cups currants

Lemon-Date Frosting:
2 cups pitted dates
4 tablespoons lemon juice
2 tablespoons lemon zest

1 lemon, cut into wedges

1. To make the bottom layer of the torte, blend the the filberts and raisins into a fine meal in a food processor fitted with an "S" blade. Press this mixture into a round shape about ½-inch thick and 8 inches in diameter.

2. Make a lemon-date frosting by pureeing the dates and lemon juice in a blender until smooth, adding a little water if needed to thin. Stir in the lemon zest.

3. Frost the top of the first layer of the torte with ½ of the frosting.

4. To make the top layer of the torte, blend the walnuts and currants into a fine meal in the food processor. Place on wax paper and press into the same size as the top layer. Carefully place on top of the frosted layer.

5. Frost the outside of the entire torte, and decorate with lemon wedges around the rim. Serve at room temperature, or warm in a dehydrator set at 105°F.

Ingredient Options: This recipe originally was prepared by Richard Salome, who is one of my favorite raw food specialists. This could be made with soaked almonds, pecans, or macadamias.

Machine Options: The Champion and Green Power machines can do this as well, using the solid "blank." A regular blender doesn't have the power to process the nuts, however a food processor or a Vita-Mix will do.

Notes

"Unbaked" Apple

Day 6

Yield: 2 servings

8 hours to soak
2 to 6 hours to dehydrate
20 minutes to prepare

The aroma of this "unbaked" apple in your home is heavenly.

2 cups organic figs
1 cup dried apricots

Sauce:
1 cup water
2 cinnamon sticks
¼ teaspoon ground cloves
¼ teaspoon ground nutmeg
1 lemon

2 organic apples

1. Soak the figs and apricots overnight, then drain and save the soaking water.

2. To make the sauce, heat the water and soak the cinnamon sticks, cloves, and nutmeg for about 20 minutes; remove the cinnamon sticks and save for garnish. In a blender, puree ½ of the soaked fruit with the spiced warmed water.

3. Pour the spiced sauce into a bowl, and dehydrate with the cored apples at 105°F for 2 to 6 hours. (The apple can sit in the sauce or be dehydrated separately.)

4. Serve warm topped with the sauce and garnished with the remaining soaked fruit and curls of cinnamon stick on top.

Ingredient Options: The sauce could be made with dates, currants, raisins, or apricots. Fujis are my favorite variety of apple—such an exquisite bouquet!

Machine Options: You could simplify this recipe by not dehydrating the apples. Just slice them and warm the slices and sauce together in an electric skillet, keeping the temperature on low. The flavors are much richer in the dehydrator, however.

Notes

Hawaiian Treats

Day 7

Yield: 20 to 30 cookies

30 minutes to prepare
4 to 10 hours to dehydrate

So rich, so worth the treat. Indulge yourself every now and then with this rich dessert.

2 cups macadamia nuts
½ apple
1 cup organic raisins

1. In a Vita-Mix or a food processor with an "S" blade, process the macadamia nuts, apple, and raisins to a smooth dough.

2. Place spoonfuls of the dough on dehydrator trays very close together, and dehydrate at 105°F for 4 to 10 hours.

Ingredient Options: Raisins are a heavily sprayed crop. Grapes can have over 86 different pesticides used on them during their growing season. It pays to find organic raisins. This dough could be made with pecans, walnuts, or soaked almonds. Currants, figs, or apricots could also be used. Ginger, cinnamon, cardamom, or nutmeg can be used to spice the treats.

Machine Options: This cookie dough is so tasty you could eat it fresh and not dehydrate it. The cookies could also be put in the sunshine and sun-"baked," turning them over once. The dough could be prepared with several machines. The Champion and Green Power machines can do this as well, using the solid "blank." A regular blender doesn't have the power to process the nuts, however a food processor or Vita-Mix will do fine.

Notes

Snack Choices

Day 1—A Dressed Naked Veggie Platter

Pick your favorite vegetables and season to your heart's content.

Crisp, sweet, succulent, fresh naked vegetables in season, lightly dressed in a lemon, flax seed oil, and Tomato Tornado dressing.

Day 2—Ricotta "Cheese" Spread with Veggie "Chips"

A fluffy almond "cheese" served with veggie "chips" made with almonds, celery, red bell pepper, and purple cabbage.

Day 3—Mexi-Flax Crisps

Flax seeds spiced with Mexican flavors and dehydrated into a tasty "crisped" cracker.

Flax seeds, garlic, tomato, red bell pepper, green onion, Mexican spice, sea salt.

Day 4—Rye Bread Sticks with Avocado Sauce

A soft, chewy rye bread stick spiced classically with caraway, playfully dipped into a spicy avocado sauce.

Bread Sticks: rye, sunflower seeds, flax seeds, caraway seeds;

Sauce: avocado, tomato, green onions, mustard.

Day 5—Ah Nuts

Crunch and munch water-rich cucumber with your favorite nut.

A cucumber and nut treat with pecans, walnuts, and/or soaked almonds.

Day 6—A Date with a Sweetie

Let nature sweeten your palate.

Apricots, dates, oranges, and strawberries—a treat to sweeten your life.

Day 7—Sunny Seed "Cheese" Dip with Jicama

A creamy/crunchy snack. Enjoy the calcium-rich fermented seed "cheese" with your choice of fresh veggies.

Sunflower seeds, garlic, onion, jicama, fresh veggies in season.

A word about snacks

Whether you like to crunch or munch, these snacks are fun to prepare and more fun to share with those who like to eat "junk." Finding your favorites can be a process that will teach you what you need at different times. Sometimes a sweet snack is just perfect. Or salty can hit the mark. Other times a soft and crunchy savory snack hits the spot. Variety is the key, and keeping the ingredients on hand, soaked and ready to prepare, will lead to a quick-to-prepare creation—what a snack is supposed to be.

Each week, plan out what you might like to snack on and soak the ingredients necessary to enjoy that particular treat. If you are doing the crackers or the seed cheeses, give yourself enough time to have them done and readily available for you when the urge to snack strikes.

Dehydrating can be a new skill you enjoy doing. There are several dehydrators on the market that you can bring into your life for preparing the crackers or cheese. The benefits of each model are personal. I enjoy the quiet of the Living Foods Dehydrator, which has no fan—only a heating element and a draw to create the air flow inside the unit. There are times when the fan of the Excalibur makes the difference between fresh and too fermented, which can happen in the absence of a fan. The size and location of the space you have to use these new machines in your life can also determine your choice. I have done several television programs on how to use a dehydrator, which have helped people see the possibilities of this marvelous tool. Whether it is crunchy munchies, like dried fruit or nuts, or more complicated recipes, enjoy the variety that your living foods kitchen can create.

A Dressed Naked Veggie Platter

Day 4

10 minutes to prepare

Munch these water-rich, vitamin- and mineral-filled foods to your heart's content.

Fresh veggies in season:
Your favorites and/or
Asparagus
Bell peppers
Broccoli
Bok choy
Cabbage
Carrots
Celery
Corn
Cucumber
Jicama
Onions: green, white, yellow, or red
Snow peas
Squash
Sugar snap peas
Yams

Dressing:
Lemon juice
Dulse
Tomato Tornado (see page 133)
Flax seed oil

1. Pick your favorite in-season vegetables, and slice into friendly, bite-sized shapes. Place in a large bowl.

2. Toss with the dressing ingredients, spicing to taste, or serve on a platter with the dressing mixed in a bowl, chip-and-dip style.

Ingredient Options: Most all of the vegetables you are used to cooking can be eaten raw, artichokes being an exception. Bok choy is amazingly water-rich. Jicama looks like it may be hard and tough, but its crisp, moist white meat is delightful. Yam chips are sweet and calcium-rich. Choose two or three of your favorites, and delight in their snack-ability.

Machine Options: A sharp knife makes slicing, dicing, mincing, and julienne cutting a pleasure. Treat yourself to a good, sharp knife.

Notes

Ricotta "Cheese" Spread with Veggie "Chips"

Day 2

Yield: 4 to 6 servings

24 hours soaking
6 to 8 hours to dehydrate
15 minutes to prepare

A fluffy nut spread with all the enzymes needed to digest it—what a deal!

"Cheese" Spread:
2 cups almonds
2 cups purified water

Veggie "Chips":
2 stalks celery
½ red bell pepper
Two 1-inch slices purple cabbage

1. Soak the almonds for 24 hours, then blanch by pouring boiling water over, rinsing, and peeling the skins off.

2. In a blender, puree the blanched almonds with the 2 cups water. Pour into a pie plate, and dehydrate at 105°F for 6 to 8 hours until it achieves a "cream cheese" consistency.

3. To make veggie "chips," slice the celery, bell pepper, and cabbage into chip shapes.

4. Serve the "cheese" warm on a platter surrounded by chips.

Ingredient Options: The "cheese" can be spiced with basil, dill weed, garlic, onions, or curry, but it tastes so fine plain, like a ricotta cheese, you may like it just as it is. Try the variations for yourself, and find your favorites. The thicker you make this "cheese," the less time it takes to dehydrate.

Machine Options: A Vita-Mix works best, but a regular blender will be fine.

Mexi-Flax Crisps

Day 3

Yield: 24 to 36 two-inch crackers

4 to 6 hours to soak
15 minutes to prepare
6 to 12 hours to dehydrate

The perfect source of crunch and omega-3 essential fatty acids.

1 cup flax seeds
1 tomato
½ red bell pepper
½ beet
1 clove garlic
1 teaspoon Mexican spice (blend of chili powder, garlic,
cumin, oregano, etc.)
1 green onion and/or ½ small red onion
Celtic salt, to taste

1. Soak the flax seeds in 2 cups water for 2 to 4 hours.

2. In a Vita-Mix or blender, briefly puree the tomato, bell pepper, beet, garlic, Mexican spice, onion, and Celtic salt—keep it chunky.

3. Stir the soaked flax seeds into the blended mixture, and spoon 2-inch rounds on a dehydrator tray covered with a teflex sheet or wax paper. Dehydrate at 105°F for 6 to 12 hours, or to the desired crispness, turning the crackers over after 4 to 6 hours.

4. Store in a plastic bag or a lidded container.

Ingredient Options: The beauty of this cracker/crisp is that it can be spiced in a wide variety of flavors: Italian, Indian curry, or a sweet variety with bananas and dates or raisins and cinnamon. Have fun finding your own versions. I enjoy using soaked seeds (such as sunflower, pumpkin, and sesame) and green leafy spices to decorate the tops of the crackers. This is best done right after you spoon the batter onto the dehydrator trays.

Machine Options: A food processor fitted with an "S" blade could be used to blend the tomato mixture as well.

Rye Bread Sticks with Avocado Sauce

Day 1

Yield: 24 to 36 six-inch bread sticks
1 to 1½ cups sauce

12 hours to soak
15 minutes to prepare
4 to 8 hours to dehydrate

Essential fatty acids, calcium, vitamins B and C—it's a whopper of a snack.

1 cup rye
⅛ cup flax seeds
⅛ cup caraway seeds
½ cup sunflower seeds
1 to 2 tablespoons Bragg Liquid Aminos

Avocado Sauce:
1 avocado
1 tomato
2 green onions
1 teaspoon mustard powder

1. Soak the rye, flax seeds, caraway seeds, and sunflower seeds together overnight. Rinse.

2. In a Vita-Mix or food processor fitted with an "S" blade, process the soaked grain and seeds together with ½ to 1 cup water. (Use less if you want a thicker bread stick; more would make a cracker.)

3. Stir in the Bragg and roll out bread sticks ½ inch in diameter and 6 to 8 inches in length. Place on dehydrator trays, and dehydrate at 105°F for 4 to 8 hours, or to the desired crispness.

4. In a blender, puree all the avocado sauce ingredients to a smooth consistency. Serve as a spicy dipping sauce for the bread sticks.

Ingredient Options: This dough could be made with barley, oat groats, wheat berries, or kamut. The spices could be Mexican, Italian, granulated garlic, minced onion, or dried parsley.

Machine Options: This dough could also be put in the sunshine and sun "baked." The Green Power Machine, with its bread stick attachment, is the easiest to use with this recipe. Combine that with the solid "blank," and you have ready-made bread sticks.

Notes

Ah Nuts

Day 5

5 minutes to prepare

A snack so simple, so sublime.

Unwaxed cucumbers
Pecans, walnuts, or soaked almonds

1. Pick your favorite raw, unsalted, unroasted, untoasted nuts, and enjoy with your favorite variety of cucumber, sliced or eaten whole.

2. Arrange on a plate or pack up for snacking while you travel.

Ingredient Options: I had no idea the wide range of cucumber varieties that are available. I went to our farmers' market and found Persian cucumbers—almost seedless; Armenian cucumbers—long, sweet, and thin; Japanese cucumbers—even longer and thinner than the Armenian, but also seedless; pickling cucumbers—short, not waxed, and few seeds; and hot house cucumbers—soft skinned and unwaxed. See what your area has to offer.

If you can only get waxed cucumbers, peel off the skin. Since most of the nutrients are in the skin, try to find them unwaxed. Encourage the produce person in your local market to carry them.

Machine Options: A sharp knife makes slicing, dicing, mincing, and julienne cutting a pleasure. Treat yourself to a good, sharp knife. This snack doesn't really even need tools; just crunch and munch to your heart's delight.

A Date with a Sweetie

Day 6

Yield: 2 servings

5 minutes to prepare

A snack so sweet with nature's most lovely colors and flavors.

4 dates (Medjool or your favorite variety)
8 dried apricots (Turkish are the best)
2 oranges
1 pint fresh strawberries

1. Pick the tastiest dried fruits and juiciest fresh oranges and strawberries. Slice into friendly, bite-sized shapes.

2. Arrange on a plate or pack up for snacking while you travel.

Ingredient Options: If you've never had Turkish apricots, find them. The fancier gourmet stores will sell them, and they are heavenly. Dates have a wide range of textures (from dry to very moist) and sweetness—some dates are not very sweet at all. Taste the different varieties and find your favorite. Strawberries contain a natural pain killer (salicylate) and make an excellent food when you have worked out just a bit too long and feel a bit too sore.

Oranges are also vastly different. From Mandarin to navel, the flavors really vary, as does the amount of juice. If an orange feels light, it probably doesn't contain much juice. It should have some weight. Navel oranges are better for eating, whereas Valencias are better for juicing.

Machine Options: A sharp knife makes slicing, dicing, mincing, and julienne cutting a pleasure. Treat yourself to a good, sharp knife. This snack doesn't really even need tools, just peel and satisfy your sweet tooth.

Sunny Seed "Cheese" Dip with Jicama

Day 7

Yield: 8 to 12 servings

12 hours to soak
8 to 12 hours to ferment
10 minutes to prepare

The perfect way to add back friendly bacteria with this naturally fermented food.

"Cheese" Dip:
4 cups sunflower seeds
4 to 6 cups purified water
1 teaspoon granulated garlic
1 onion, minced

Veggie "Chips":
Sliced jicama
Sliced veggies, fresh and in season

1. Soak the sunflower seeds for 12 hours; rinse.

2. In a blender, process all the "cheese" dip ingredients, adding enough water to thin the mixture. The more water, the larger the volume of seed cheese.

3. Pour the mixture into a large, widemouthed glass jar, and cover with a cloth napkin or clean dish cloth. Leave on the counter overnight, and let ferment into seed "cheese."

4. Serve the "cheese" at room temperature, or chill and serve on a platter surrounded by jicama "chips" (or any other crunchy vegetable you like).

Ingredient Options: The "cheese" can be spiced with basil, dill weed, garlic, onions, or curry. Find your favorites. The thicker you make this, the less time it takes to ferment. This cheese likes to ferment in a warm place, but not in direct sun. If you want to make this more like a farmers' cheese, strain the mixture in cheese cloth, drain or squeeze out the moisture, chill, and serve. It keeps for at least 3 to 5 days refrigerated.

Machine Options: A Vita-Mix works best, but a regular blender is fine.

Notes

Drink Choices

Day 1—Blushing Garden Juice

A tonic for the blood, great for healthy hair and nails, this is a juice for all seasons.

Carrots, beets, celery, cucumber, lemon.

Day 2:—"Sun" Teas

Herb teas warmed by the sun, a plethora of teas to choose from.

Day 3—Lean Green Juice

A calcium- and chlorophyll-rich juice, all green and so sweet, built to help us last a long time.

Romaine lettuce, parsley, spinach, cucumber, celery, apples.

Day 4—A Berry Delicious Drink

A refreshing, thirst-quenching drink for those hot, dry days.

Strawberries, raspberries, bananas, orange juice, dates.

Day 5—Pineapple Delight

A delicate blend of unexpected and uncommonly tasty flavors, great for digestion and chlorophyll.

Pineapple, cilantro, green leaf lettuce, lime.

Day 6—Orange You Glad We've Got Omega-3 Oils Blend?

What a tasty way to reduce cholesterol and build your bones—a toast to your health.

Orange juice, flax seeds, romaine lettuce.

Day 7—Banini Shake:

One of the sweetest ways to put more calcium and potassium into your diet—a drink for us all.

Tahini (sesame seed "butter"), bananas, dates.

A word about drinks

Getting enough liquid into our bodies every day is so important. Some people believe that other than air, water is one of the most important nutrients, necessary to create health. Although water is not mentioned as a drink in this section, it is the most obvious beverage choice available to us every day. Fewer and fewer of us can enjoy the luxury of pure, delicious, untreated water from our own wells or springs, so investigate the many devices available on the market for treating the water you drink. Whether it is RO (reverse osmosis), distilled, or filtered water, we all need to rehydrate our bodies every day.

Sun teas are such a treat, and if there is no sun, these teas can be made on your kitchen counter—they are still delicious. There are a world of fresh juices to choose from, and there are markets now that sell freshly processed juices, not just the pasteurized, sugar-filled choices that are labeled "juice drink." Going to the movies with a jug of sun tea sure helps avoid the temptation to order a soda, which is one of the most harmful drinks we can choose. Destroying my bones is not my idea of a good time, and the phosphorous content in sodas contributes to the imbalance of minerals that leeches calcium from our bones and makes it unusable. Nice to have better choices.

Blending foods together to make a drink is so tasty, and you are getting the benefit of the full food in a liquid form. Find the combinations you like best, whether they are flax or a fresh date blended into juice. Blending greens into your drinks makes some of the sweetness more palatable for those of us "sugar babies" in recovery.

Transporting your drinks in a thermos can insure the temperature and freshness of your choice. Otherwise, there are days when I put a cooler in my car with a freshly frozen ice pack to keep my drinks and food cool during transport in the desert on those more than warm summer days.

Find the drinks that you enjoy, make them, and have them ready to serve. Warming can be a simple task in the Vita-Mix, or it can be done by adding warm water to the drinks before serving or sitting the poured drinks in a tub of warm water.

You too can make your drink and enjoy its benefits—a toast to your health.

Blushing Garden Juice

Day 1

Yield: 2 servings

10 minutes to prepare

Juice your salad for a smoother swallow.

6 to 8 carrots
1 beet
2 beet green leaves
2 stalks celery
½ unwaxed cucumber
1 lemon, cut in wedges

1. Juice the carrots, beet, greens, celery, and cucumber together.

2. Serve in fancy glasses, running some cut lemon around the rim of each glass and garnishing with a lemon wedge.

Ingredient Notes: Cucumbers can be found unwaxed even in regular markets. Usually they are the pickling or hot house variety. The skin of the cucumber has most of the nutrients in it, so it behooves one to eat or juice an unwaxed cucumber. To quote Norman Walker, cucumbers "contain more than 40% potassium, 10% sodium, 7½% calcium, 20% phosphorous, and 7% chlorine." They are quite a good choice as a natural diuretic—promoting the excretion and flow of urine—and in combination with carrot and beet juice, cucumber juice is also a lovely tonic for menopause.

I enjoy this on a cool morning, and this combination can certainly be served before lunch or dinner. Juices are absorbed so quickly by our systems. The best way to savor a juice is to "chew" it first in your mouth to activate the salivary process of digestion. On an empty stomach, juices absorb through the stomach lining, taking much less energy to digest.

Beets and their greens are a great liver cleanser, and lemon juice stimulates the liver to make enzymes. So this is a good liver toning drink.

"Sun" Teas

Day 2

Yield: 1 quart

10 minutes to prepare
1 to 4 hours to "brew"

Tease your tea with a kiss of sunlight.

Herb teas (some of my favorites are Cinnamon Spice, Blackberry Forest, Spearmint, and Cranberry Iced Delight) 1 quart purified water

1. In an empty quart jar, put 2 to 4 tea bags of your favorite herb tea, fill with purified water, and place in a window or outside in the sun. Wait until "brewed."

2. Serve in fancy glasses.

Ingredient Notes: Celestial Seasonings, Aavita, and Seelect have a wide range of herb teas that are delightful for making into "sun" tea. One winter, with no sun in sight, I decided to make a quart of "sun" tea. I left it out on the counter for a couple of hours, and around lunch time I tasted it—it was just fine. Sun tea can be made without the sun, but I prefer the taste of warmed tea.

On very hot days, make a batch of sun tea and cool it with ice cubes or cooled juice. Apple juice blends very well with many herb teas.

Lean Green Juice

Day 3

Yield: 2 servings

10 minutes to prepare

Great greens to drink at any time.

2 leaves romaine lettuce
2 to 3 apples
2 stalks celery
½ cup parsley
1 unwaxed cucumber
½ cup spinach

1. Juice all the ingredients together.

2. Serve in fancy glasses.

Ingredient Notes: To really make this a chlorophyll-rich drink, add spirulina, available at most health food stores. Spirulina has many special benefits including reducing the risk of cancer.

If you want even more calcium in this drink, add carrot juice to taste.

Glorious Garden Hi-Pro "Fundue" with Veggie "Chips," pages 42-43